W9-CPC-864
4012.
K58

THE KNUBEL-MILLER FOUNDATION
of The United Lutheran Church in America
Sixth Series of Lectures

Pastoral Counseling

By
FREDERICK R. KNUBEL
President, United Lutheran Synod of New York and New England

THE BOARD OF PUBLICATION
OF THE UNITED LUTHERAN CHURCH IN AMERICA
PHILADELPHIA, PENNSYLVANIA

COPYRIGHT 1952, BY
THE BOARD OF PUBLICATION OF
THE UNITED LUTHERAN CHURCH IN AMERICA

Printed in U. S. A.

CONTENTS

I

WHAT IS THE PASTORAL COUNSELING MOVEMENT?

Ointment and perfume rejoice the heart; so doth the sweetness of a man's friend by hearty counsel. PROVERBS 27:9

It is a double honor to be chosen to present the Knubel-Miller Lectures, for not only are they of influence in the church but they are partly in my father's memory. That memory places upon me a heavy weight of responsibility to do it justice. Yet it also makes the task one of exhilaration because of my gratitude for all that my father meant to me, and because of his lifelong conviction of the importance of pastoral ministration. No two other men were more absorbed in the activity and welfare of parish work than Dr. E. Clarence Miller and my father.

Nevertheless for a long time I was reluctant to accept the responsibility of speaking on the subject of pastoral counseling because I knew that there were others more competent, by special training and clinical experience. I was told, however, that an objective examination of the modern pastoral counseling movement was desired, on the basis of my twenty-three years' experience as a pastor in an active parish, and seven more as a pastor of pastors, which is the chief function of the president of a synod. Furthermore, it had become a pressing necessity for me to give alert attention to the subject, because of the increasing number of young men coming under the synod's direction as graduate students majoring in it. The seminaries which are controlled by the synods were also groping, and I felt I had to grope with them.

The immense popularity of the subject intrigued me. It seemed to be reaching the fever of a fad in the body of the church, but I knew that in the past many good and permanent things had come out of such enthusiasms. "Pastoral Counseling" was first on the list of requests from pastors for this lectureship—so predominantly that there was almost no second choice. Nevertheless I found that many of my fellow pastors knew as little about it as I. So in my office of helping pastors I concluded that if I really studied up on it I might be of aid to them. I read all I could find, interviewed many who had had clinical training, consulted leaders and teachers, doctors and ministers, and in general buttonholed everybody I met on the subject. My first conclusion is that I have still very much to learn. In these lectures I have to make a very brash assumption (one which I realize is not true of many who hear me), namely that you are as ignorant of the subject as I was when I took up the study. I only hope that you will reap some of the benefit I have found, and if it is an old story to you that you will come to the help of the rest of us during the important discussion periods.

PASTORAL COUNSELING IS PSYCHOTHERAPY

The first discovery I made was that pastoral counseling, in the current sense of the term, is psychotherapy. As Dr. Anton Boisen, a father of the movement, has written, "The term 'counseling' is the non-medical equivalent of 'psychotherapy.' " [1] It springs out of the modern widespread cult of "dynamic" psychology, which in turn stems from Freud.

Freud investigated and dramatized two great realities: the importance of the unconscious and the importance of the emotions. Conscious behavior, evident to the observer, is motivated hugely by hidden unconscious urges, as well as by repressed conflicts among those urges and with one's conscience. What is needed, therefore, for the relief of disturbances such as fear, anxiety, hostility, self-withdrawal, frustration, depression, guilt feeling, and general unhappiness is to get these hidden urges and conflicts out into the open, face them squarely, and resolve them into positive and constructive directions.

So fruitful have such procedures been, especially in cases dealt with in the world wars, that a whole modern general movement has resulted which has touched every field of human endeavor. Counseling services have been provided by colleges, vocational guidance centers, the Veteran's Administration, big business corporations, social agencies, and even a faltering major-league baseball team. They are aimed at the unconscious and the emotions. I need hardly remind my hearers how this enthusiasm and popular appeal have spread to magazines, books, newspapers, radio, and television. One single newspaper page before me at this moment, for instance, has the following departments: "Everyday Counselor," "The Worry Clinic," "Looking at Life," "Everyday Problems," and "Mirror of Your Mind." Among doctors a new field has developed called psychosomatic medicine, and medical students are given increased instruction on the interaction between emotions and bodily functions. Indeed, the chief textbook in this subject ends with the sentence, "The mind is the body and the body is the mind." [2]

In the church the movement took hold in 1923 by what is

now known as Clinical Pastoral Training. Students and pastors under supervision studied cases in mental hospitals, taking notes on their conferences with patients and presenting reports. General hospitals and correctional institutions have now been added, so that pastors can "come into firsthand contact with deeper levels of personality," and "rub shoulders with specific instances of human difficulty." Seminaries, including some of our own, have been intimately tied up with this effort, and all are adding to their curriculum.

The dangers of this movement, for pastors, seem to be threefold. The first is that they will be swallowed up by a fad. There is no doubt that modern "dynamic" psychology is in the fad stage. That is inevitable in any movement of potential value when it is exaggerated, when its wild claims have not yet been clinically established, and when it is distorted by popular misapplication. Specifically, the overenthusiastic pastor is in danger of considering every parishioner as a classified "case," whose supposed hidden motivations may actually not exist at all.

This leads to a second danger: that because of reading and study the pastor shall count himself a kind of psychiatrist, spending too much time in "counseling" in relation to other duties, experimenting on the precious souls God has given him, pridefully elated at supposed cures, and finally abandoning the specific functions of the Christian ministry, as many have done.

The greatest danger, however, is that the pastor shall limit himself within the restrictions of scientific methodology which by definition casts out any hint of divine intervention, religious autonomy, or sacred revelation. The pastor, whatever helpful use he gets, and should get, from psychology, must be above all the servant of the divine Saviour Jesus Christ and the minister of Christ's revealed Word and instituted sacraments.

In this ministry, and with the above warnings, I believe that the pastor can gratefully use many of the insights of modern psychological investigation. Indeed, can his ministry be as effective as it ought to be if he does not? Suppose, for instance, that a pastor is called to the bedside of the engineer whose case is related by Karen Horney in her book, *Our Inner Conflicts.*[3] He was in a state of complete exhaustion and depression. Such a condition is sometimes very simple: just a matter of overwork and bodily misfunction, and as such calls for sympathy, prayer, friendliness, and the comfort of the Scriptures. But this case was more complicated. It seems that at the construction company office, this engineer's opinions were less well received, on a certain technical matter, than those of his colleagues. Also, he had not been consulted on a certain company decision. Instead of putting up a fight or else accepting the majority decision with good grace, he harbored a hidden, unconscious, murderous rage which appeared only in his dreams. This repressed rage—a composite of his fury against the others and of his fury against himself for his own meekness—was mainly responsible for his fatigue. A number of factors were back of his failure to act reasonably and consistently. He had unconsciously built up a grandiose image of himself that required deference from others to support it. Furthermore, he had unconscious sadistic impulses to berate and humiliate others—an attitude so objectionable to himself that he covered it up by overfriendliness. To this was added an unconscious drive to exploit people, making it imperative for him to keep in their good graces. The dependence on others was aggravated by a compulsive need for approval and affection and therefore avoidance of a fight. The result was inner upheaval that went on unrealized either by himself or anybody else. How much more effectively could the pastor have ministered to him if the pastor had somehow been able to get these sinful things out into the open. How harmful might some of his ministration otherwise be!

The point is that when people come to us with problems, there is often something much deeper than the problem itself. A mother will come to the pastor for help in disciplining her child, when actually the trouble may lie in the fact that she never wanted the child but has repressed the fact and is not conscious of it. Let the pastor beware because such hidden influences may never actually exist. But let him keep alert for them, especially where there is unreasonable and unusual emotional evidence. The investigations of modern psychology have often served to underline the Christian truths of original sin and deep selfishness, and the tree as the real cause of the evil fruit. "Who can understand his sins? cleanse thou me from secret faults." "The heart is deceitful above all things." "Keep well thy heart, for out of it are the issues of life."

PSYCHOTHERAPY IS NONDIRECTIVE COUNSELING

My second discovery concerning the pastoral counseling movement was that it is confined largely to a single method of psychotherapy known as "nondirective counseling." This technique is accounted as the best to bring out hidden difficulties. It is based on an entirely secular book by Carl R. Rogers, *Counseling and Psychotherapy.* Rogers did not discover the method but has developed it far more systematically than anyone else.

"Nondirective counseling" (or as Rogers terms it in a later book, "client-centered counseling") consists of three stages. First, there is the release of expression by the client. He is encouraged to talk without interruption and on whatever he desires. The chief attitude of the counselor is acceptance. The counselor is never shocked, censorious, moralistic, or probing. He never gives advice. He never even expresses a judgment, good or bad, lest he hinder the flow of free expression. The client need never feel on the defensive. From start to finish, the counselor never takes one shred of responsibility except to be sure that all responsibility rests upon the client. This is made clear to the client before the counseling process begins.

What, then, does the counselor say? Frequently he gives only a murmur of understanding and acceptance. At other times he gives simply a reflection of what the client has said, often in the client's own words. Sometimes he rephrases the client's words, not for the sake of the counselor's understanding but of the client's. The response of the counselor is to the feeling and emotions which the client shows, rather than to the content of the words. There must be no hint of authority and no rebuke, admonition, coercion, argument, explanation, exhortation—or generalization. No assurances are given, no words of comfort or cheer, no optimistic prophecies. Furthermore, the counselor is not primarily concerned with the problem which the client has, but with the client himself and what he feels. The counselor is not solving the problem for the client, but bringing out the client so that he can solve his own problem. From the start there must be a warmth and responsiveness on the part of the counselor which make rapport possible and which gradually induce a deeper emotional relationship, always under the counselor's control. Everything is done to get the client to verbalize his emotions, on the theory that "most maladjustments are not failures in knowing, but that knowledge is ineffective because it is blocked by the emotional satisfactions" which the individual accumulates through his present maladjustments.

This continues, for about an hour, at intervals of several days, often for many weeks, during which time the client gradually achieves insight into his own hidden motives and feelings, an experience that comes with great rapidity and spontaneity toward the end of the treatment. He sees old facts in new relationships. This is the conclusion of the second phase of the method.

Here, for instance, is a mother talking about her struggles to keep her handicapped boy in health and make him learn.[4]

> CLIENT: "Maybe I haven't tried hard enough."
>
> COUNSELLOR: "Maybe you've tried too hard."
>
> CLIENT: "I don't know, I don't know. I went to this baby specialist, and he asked me two questions, and then he said to me, 'Well, take him home and let him be,' and I said, 'If there is something wrong with him, why don't you tell me the truth? (Voice rising to crescendo.) I'd like to know the truth, and then I would know exactly how to go about it and know that I've got to make up my mind, and I'll hire him out for a carpenter or cement mixer or something! Tell me the truth—!"
>
> COUNSELOR: (sympathetically): "Don't you know the truth already?"
>
> CLIENT (very quietly—voice very much changed): "I don't want to know it. I don't want to believe it. I don't want to know it." (Tears come to her eyes.)

Bit by bit, there is gradual increase in self-understanding.

Recognition and acceptance of self comes. Defenses are down. Release has come, and something happens that is very close to confession and conversion.

The third stage is positive action resulting from insight. "If the new orientation is not spontaneously reinforced by action, it is obvious that it has not deeply involved the personality." But again these actions must be entirely self-initiated, with no suggestion on the part of the counselor, so that responsibility still rests entirely upon the client. The continuation of this third phase, in Rogers' book, is essentially beyond the professional counselor's sphere, and very few pages are devoted to it. It is all up to the client.

The essentials of this method have been taken over in their entirety by Seward H. Hiltner[5] and Carroll A. Wise, the writers of two recent books, each entitled, *Pastoral Counseling.*

By way of an introduction into the method, I present a very much condensed version of an interview given in its fullness in Carroll A. Wise's book.[6]

> Jane is a young woman of twenty-two. She was not known to the counselor before coming voluntarily with a problem. This material is from the second interview.
>
> JANE: I have felt very much better this week. I have discovered that when I feel blue I don't try to snap out of it. I don't do anything to help myself. I just go on feeling blue. I don't live up to my own standards. I should do something about it, but I don't. That gets me down.
>
> COUNSELOR: You get discouraged because you don't do as you feel you should.
>
> JANE: Take smoking for example. I don't approve of smoking. But still I do it. Then I feel bad because I do it. But I don't stop doing it.
>
> COUNSELOR: Feeling bad doesn't help you change it.
>
> JANE: That's right. I think the trouble is that I have no goal

in life. Sometimes I feel it is a matter of security. I have never felt I had a home, that is, a real home. I had a place to live. But I never felt my parents cared for me.

COUNSELOR: It seems it has something to do with not having a goal and not feeling secure and loved at home?

JANE: I have taken full responsibility for myself since I was in high school. They don't care what I do. They have no interest in me. I am completely on my own. And I can't see any future in my job.

COUNSELOR: You have to look after yourself completely, and now you see nothing to look forward to.

JANE: I have nothing to look forward to. Most girls my age look forward to marriage. I suppose I should too, but I can't seem to. Yet I wish I could. But I don't want a marriage like my parents. All they ever did was fight. I have read books that said that children of unhappy parents never have happy marriages themselves. I know I don't have a chance.

COUNSELOR: Your experience with your parents and what the books say have left you pretty discouraged about your possibilities for a happy marriage.

JANE: I know I don't have a chance. My ideals are too high. I know that too. I demand perfection from others. Yet I am far from perfect. I wouldn't have enough to offer the kind of a man I want. Sometimes I get so that I want to hit something and scream at the top of my lungs.

COUNSELOR: Part of your discouragement is in your high ideals and sometimes it makes you want to let it out rather forcefully?

JANE: I give in to my moods easily. I do nothing about them. I keep blaming myself. I see that the solution lies in my own hands, but I'm not doing anything about it.

COUNSELOR: The solution is in your hands, but you do nothing about it; you feel you are letting yourself down.

JANE: That's it. I always feel lost in a crowd, or in groups. The groups at the church. I feel better in a big group than in a smaller one. No one really feels close in a big group. But a small one—I don't feel I belong.

COUNSELOR: You don't feel at home in a small group.

At this point the period was ended and another appointment was made. In future interviews the counselor may face a problem in giving her enough security to go on with the process of exploring her problem. There is a strong tendency to take a submissive reaction and let life defeat her. But there is also resistance to this. She needs security without pressure.

Now let us go back for a moment to the first words of the interview, as Wise does, and ask what you or I might have responded. Or rather, let us ask how Jane would have felt about our response.

JANE: I have felt very much better this week. I have discovered that when I feel blue I don't try to snap out of it. I don't do anything to help myself. I just go on feeling blue. I don't live up to my own standards. I should do something about it, but I don't. That gets me down.

Consider the following possible responses.

1) "Since you know what the trouble is, you should be able to do something about it."

This is moralistic, appealing also to an internal strength which Jane does not possess. If she could do this, she would not need the counselor.

2) "That is because your negative feelings are stronger than your positive feelings."

This is a psychological interpretation of the intellectual type, which explains Jane's predicament in a certain way, but does little to help her with her feelings.

3) "Evidently you don't really want to live up to your standards."

This identifies Jane with her negative feelings, says that they are stronger than her positive feelings and that therefore they represent her real self. It is an ego-deflating kind of response. It would very likely bring hostility. It indicates that the counselor has little faith in the counselee.

4) "I am very anxious to help you with this."

This response indicates exactly what it says, that the counselor is anxious. As a psychiatrist has well said, "There cannot be two anxious people in a therapeutic situation."

What the counselor actually responded was, "You get discouraged because you don't do as you feel you should." He aimed simply at accepting and reflecting her feelings. That was the purpose of every response he made. There was no judgment, comment, or generalization. The object was to help Jane express herself freely, and thereby ultimately cure herself independently.

THE IMPLICATIONS OF NONDIRECTIVE COUNSELING

It will become immediately apparent to my hearers that the *strict* and *wide* application of the nondirective method must not only exclude revelation (and therefore all Scripture), judgment (and therefore the power of the keys), and authority (and therefore the lordship of the divine Christ), but must actually declare them destructive of cure. For the heart of the method is that everything comes out of the parishioner, who cures and directs himself. Since it is the counselor who brings about this desired end, he must consider himself *in loco Dei,* although the thought would horrify him.

We must therefore examine some of the implications of the method, its theory and its assumptions, in order to use it in any way as Christian pastors. Let us do so practically, psychologically, and theologically.

1. *Practically*

The method is avowedly limited to situations where hidden emotions are dominant, and where the trouble is not in the problem presented but in the person who has the problem. Furthermore, it is a requisite that the person come to the counselor voluntarily. Few situations are as simple as this in the work of the Christian pastor.

There are many behavior problems that do not require psychological experience or extensive treatment, even when the parishioner shows disturbed emotions. Sometimes simple directions suffice: to get a job, to stop thinking of one's self constantly, to cultivate better social habits, to smile more, to stop trying to become the center of attention, or to have teeth fixed.

On the train coming to one of these lectures, I sat next to a man who was emotionally disturbed. He could not sit still. He itched and squirmed and broke out into heavy perspiration. He repeatedly got up, walked the length of the car, and sat down again. Finally he turned to me and said, "Could I ask you a question?" I was wearing clerical clothes. I thought, here is a setting for nondirective counseling. "Certainly," I replied. "Well," he said, "I know how to figure percentage from the bottom up but not from the top down. I'm a shoe salesman and I have to figure profit based on cost; but when I have that, I do not know how to figure profit based on the selling price. Can you help me out?" So I dug down into eighth-grade arithmetic and came up with the solution, and all his symptoms vanished. Suppose I had done nothing but accept and reflect his questions in true nondirective fashion? The method is not intended for such situations, but the pastor has many like them. And his use of Scripture, of the gospel, of revelation, of the principles of Jesus still remains his most important resource.

Again, sometimes a parishioner may need a direct persuasion against a course of action which he has hit upon in the course of gaining insight through nondirective counseling. It may be potentially dangerous. For instance, a parishioner, as a result of "insight," might adopt a plan of extramarital experimentation that would wreck his soul and the lives of others. Indeed, if the intended action were of an immoral and unethical nature the counselor might even become involved in the compounding of a felony or as an accessory after the fact.

2. *Psychologically*

Jung cites the case of a sour, crabbed, and intolerant vestryman who after many years suddenly sat up in bed one night and said to his wife, "Now at last I've got it. I'm just a plain rascal." Nor did this self-realization remain without results, for he spent his remaining years in riotous living and the wasting of a fortune.[7] Insight into oneself is not enough, even if acted upon.

Dr. R. Sutherland Bonnell writes in his book, *Psychiatry for Pastor and People,* of a man who came to him saying that a psychoanalyst had just declared him cured. "Then why do you come to me?" asked Dr. Bonnell." "Well, the psychoanalyst said to me 'Now you are under your own steam,' and I find I don't have any steam."[8]

When it comes to adopting an aim in life, and sometimes even a course of action, it must be Christ who points the way, and not merely the inner thoughts of the human soul. Countless are the times when a pastor must thus direct his sheep, under the great Shepherd.

Many of the above considerations, as well as some of a technical, psychological nature, will be found in A. H. Brayfield's *Readings in Modern Methods of Counseling,* where eminent teachers, while praising the work of Rogers, point out its serious limitations.[9]

Three strictures are especially important in their judgment of the method: that it has not been sufficiently tested clinically, that it does not go deep enough because it eliminates diagnosis and manipulation so as to cure only symptoms, and that it is not really nondirective because the most important element of its effectiveness is the relationship between the counselor and the counselee.

3. *Theologically*

It seems to me that there is no theological objection to the method of nondirective counseling so long as it is restricted to limited situations as above indicated, and so long as no question of real guilt is involved. Even in the latter case it can be of certain valuable help. Yet these restrictions are so important in the work of the pastor that I believe the method can seldom be used in its full and antiseptic form, as so many of its advocates insist it must be.

The real theological trouble comes when writers like Hiltner, Wise, Dicks, and most of the others insist upon making this method cover everything in theological thought and everything in parish life. I wish they would not do this. I am reminded of the delegate on the floor of a convention of the United Lutheran Church some years ago, who in the course of debate cried out, "Mr. President! This is all right as far as it goes, but it goes too far!" Within limits it is a helpful method. But in the first place it is pure science, which cannot cover all the work of the church and must eliminate all thought of revelation and the supernatural. Many of its extreme exponents have therefore honestly left parish work or the ministry itself, and have become consulting psychologists. And in the second place, some of its enthusiasts have turned it into a religion, a substitute for the gospel. They have become dissatisfied with the faith of the church as it is and has been through the ages, especially concerning authority, judgment, and autonomous divine influence. An important and insidious danger to Christianity therefore lies in the capture of the movement by such forces. It will make the movement sterile. There are signs of healthy reaction.

What I have sorrowfully in mind, because I think they are good men and are doing good, is illustrated by a few quotations from the most popular writers on pastoral counseling.

Wise writes theologically "The question is often raised, 'Where is God brought into the counseling situation?' . . . If the situation is one where the basic relationship [between counselor and counselee] is that of love in the sense of seeking the fulfillment of the personality of the counselee, then God does not have to be brought into the situation; God is in the situation."[10] "To know oneself is to know God [sic] . . . The Christian belief that man is a son of God implies that the deeper we understand the nature of man the deeper we understand the nature of God."[11] This, of course, is plain humanism or pantheism. No special revealed knowledge of God is necessary for pastor or parishioner. As Prof. Karl Heim has stated,

"If we assume that . . . God is immediately given with our own existence, there would be no need for any particular effort to seek God in prayer."[12] And such proves to be the case with Wise, who says, "The counseling process itself is a form of prayer. Where one person is seeking the truth about himself with the aid of another, there is prayer."[13] Consequently, both Hiltner and Wise deal with prayer largely in terms of cautions against it, as they deal also with Scripture.

It is Anton T. Boisen, however, who really speaks out. His fascinating book, rising out of his own recovery from insanity, and going straight to the heart of the matter, entitled *The Exploration of the Inner World,* contains this declaration of war: "I hold that the shift from faith in a revealed religion to an empirical basis . . . must be not merely accepted but eagerly furthered."[14] Dr. Boisen is the real father, and present-day Nestor, of the pastoral counseling movement in the United States.

Hiltner, in his *Pastoral Counseling* admits that there should be an ethical and a Christian-theological approach to pastoral counseling as well as an "eductive" (nondirective) approach, but he makes them melt into it, and disappear from then on. Ethics proves to be only the "similarities in the deepest level of inner need . . . in all kinds of cultures and people." In other words, it is what might come out of counseling nondirectively with all the people of the earth — nothing higher than man. He calls the body of ethics "certain minimum personality demands as being objective or existential or created part of essential human nature" — in other words, the findings of nondirective counseling on a grand scale.

As for the "Christian-theological approach," that suffers an even worse fate. It is called a "corollary" of the above ethical approach. "There is in Christian theology an undergirding for what has been stated above . . . When [the pastor] sees positive potentialities emerging from a hitherto confused and divided personality, he identifies their source as the operation of the Holy Spirit or of Divine grace."[15]

Most important, theologically and practically, is the relation of nondirective counseling (and the science of psychology generally) to the question of guilt and the forgiveness of sins. This central point is viewed in the next lecture.

ADVANTAGES TO THE PASTOR

When nondirective counseling is taken as a method for selective Christian use — not as a be-all and end-all, not as a substitute for the gospel, not as the ultimate basis for the construction of Christian doctrine and ethics, and not as the chief aim of the ministry—it can be employed with great benefit by the pastor. We owe our gratitude to those whose researches have opened up its importance and possibilities.

In the first place, it seems undoubtedly true that to a large extent the mind has the power to cure itself, just as the body has. About half of the patients in mental hospitals get better, if just given the chance by quiet and love and understanding. Many people who are not insane, but nevertheless mentally distressed and disturbed, and who come to a pastor for help, can get better just by his firm love and understanding kindness.

In the second place, most pastors talk too much and listen too little. I believe that if I had known more about nondirective counseling in my ministry, I could have been much more effective. Sometimes, in our pastoral counseling, all that people need is someone to listen—that is absolutely all. Their thinking clarifies in the process, and they begin to look at themselves objectively. All the bitterness frequently ends up in confessing faults and making allowances for the opposition. Such opening-up should not be disturbed by the pastor's ideas, moralizing, generalizing, and immediate criticizing. He should not jump in quickly with conclusions. Not all parishioners, however, should be allowed to "talk out" at length. For a depressed person to do so might result in suicide. And certain types of neurotics, who enjoy their troubles and miseries, are only made worse. But these are the exceptions. It is safe to say that ninety per cent of those who come to the pastor for counseling need listening-to above all, especially in the initial stage of the counseling. And here the pastor has immense advantage over the professional psychologist. If he is the right kind of pastor his people know that he will be both loving and just, that his love for them is rooted even deeper than any personal attractiveness on their part or any professional zeal on his: namely in his consecration to One who would not break the bruised reed nor quench the smoking flax, who gave himself in holy love, and who came to preach the gospel to the poor, deliverance to the captives and recovering of sight to the blind. Those in need found in Him acceptance, clarification, and release. And they know today that they will find it also in a real Christian shepherd.

In the third place, Lutherans—who correctly put right doctrine first simply because it safeguards and eases the mental grasp of the loving gospel of Christ—need to remind themselves often that (according to their own doctrine) faith in the Word and not the intellectual grasp of theology is the basis of salvation, and that sometimes the Word has to wait until people are ready for it. Jesus said to his disciples, "I have yet many things to say unto you, but ye cannot bear them now. Howbeit when he, the Spirit of truth, is come, he will guide you into all truth." The Spirit does his work through the Word, and I therefore differ from the enthusiasts of nondirective counseling when they say that the Word can never be given except before or after the "counseling process." The Word is not mere intellectualizing. But I realize that argument and logic are always useless until the emotional background is laid, until the parishioner has been given the chance to let out his feelings, and often until some of the inner conflict has been brought out and faced.

Finally, in the counseling process, a pastor should realize that it is always a matter of the parishioner and Christ, not of the parishioner and pastor. What brings the parishioner and Christ together is not the pastor but the Spirit. It is the Spirit's work, not the pastor's. That realization will keep him from personal, officious interfering and also from personal anxiety. It will make him respect the integrity and value of the soul in its dealing with God. It will keep the pastor from coercion, moralizing, rationalizing, and philosophizing. It will take all pride out of his heart and also all fear. It will make him content to listen and understand, and to let the Word do its work in season.

II

HOW MUCH PSYCHOLOGY SHOULD A PASTOR KNOW?

Who is this that darkeneth counsel by words without knowledge?
JOB 38:2

Counsel is darkened when the pastor shuts his eyes to the science of psychology and the psychologist shuts his eyes to God.

It is impossible to say to psychology, "You stay in your field," and to religion, "You stay in yours." The fields overlap. They both deal with personality and with interpersonal relations. Great words are common to both: mind, heart, soul, spirit, faith, hope, love, hate, desire, self, aim, guilt, fear, happiness, destiny, character.

THE LIMITATIONS OF PSYCHOLOGY

The difficulty that psychology encounters in the use of these sublime words is twofold. In the first place, psychology claims to be a science, and these things do not lend themselves easily to experiment, prediction, and control. They get lost in the process. As Allport says, "You cannot experiment with embarrassment, remorse, falling in love, or religious ecstasy." [1] As for personality, every person is different. When you have a set of laws concerning humanity in general you do not necessarily have anything about John Smith who is in front of you for pastoral counseling. He baffles science.

In the second place, psychology works its cures ultimately

by leading the person to something to live for; but it has a hard time determining what that is, and can of itself provide no motive power beyond a refined form of selfishness. It cannot therefore succeed on its own ground alone.

Take for instance the goals usually posited by psychology: maturity, growth, integration, adjustment, and peace of mind. What is maturity? Cynicism is a form of it, and many "mature" people need Jesus' words, "Except ye . . . become as little children, ye shall not enter into the kingdom of heaven." Growth? What kind? Cancer is growth. Integration? Around what? Hitler, I suppose, was one of the most completely integrated personalities that ever existed. So is Satan. And adjustment to what? Appeasement is a form of adjustment. So is promiscuity or extramarital experience, actually advised by some psychologists. As for "peace of mind," that may just be a good description of an alligator in the mud, or of death, or of out-and-out evil. As the editor of a popular mind-cure magazine recently had to confess, "Anybody who is happy today ought to have his head examined." Religion, writes Hocking, "declares the soul most in need of healing when it is most satisfied with itself, and is likely to regard the beginning of anxiety as the first stage toward recovery from mortal danger." [2]

The most eminent psychologists, I find, fully realize this limitation, and do one of two things. Either they admit (like Allport of Harvard) that the psychologist and his patient need common sense, intuition, and above all God; or else (like Erich Fromm) they proceed to evolve a religion of their own.[3] This turns out to be plain humanism, resulting in the favorite ultimate of many therapists: that if you can persuade a patient to love himself, he will automatically love others. On the contrary, testifies our own Dr. Paul Morentz, the "psyched" are always more selfish than they were before, unless they have something beyond psychoanalysis: a dominant passion for something outside of themselves which is real.

The most respected experts in the field also have a modesty about psychology which is far different from the brash claims of many of their popularizers and followers. Wechsler of Columbia humbly writes, "It is no discredit to psychology to acknowledge that it has barely emerged from the descriptive stage—more of an art than a science." [4] And Sullivan went so far as to declare, "Psychiatry as it is . . . is not science nor art but confusion." [5]

In the light of these limitations upon psychology, both as it now is and as it ever can be, how unwise it is for a pastor to come under its complete domination. Possessing Christ, the Word, and the Holy Spirit, he ministers a salvation which is both earthly and heavenly. He can use psychology as a helpful servant, but when it becomes his master it not only disintegrates his ministry but even defeats the aims of his psychology itself. Far greater than "dynamic" psychology, the pastor has the gospel which is the dynamite of God for salvation to the lowest and most despairing, and which is for all people: Jew and Gentile, male and female, bond and free.

THE PASTOR'S NEED

How much psychology, then, should a pastor know? It hardly needs to be said: not enough to make him morbid and not enough to make him think he is an expert psychiatrist, though our men have sometimes fallen into both of these dangers. Profound study in this field (or perhaps superficial study, even more) is necessarily introspective and can warp minds. As the old jingle has it:

> The centipede was happy, quite,
> Until the toad, for fun
> Said, "Pray which leg comes after which?"
> This worked her mind to such a pitch
> She lay distracted in a ditch,
> Considering how to run.

Dr. Harvey Hoover warns, "Dabbling in psychiatry, psychotherapy, and other fields requiring the services of experts is not only dangerous and disastrous, it is untrue to . . . the ministry."

Yet Dr. Hoover and the Lutheran teachers of practical theology before him have never been obscurantists. Witness the teaching of the late Dr. G. H. Gerberding, in his *Lutheran Pastor* published fifty years ago: "The pastor needs to understand human nature in all its diversified forms and phases. And here a wide field of research opens to him. What is the influence of the body on the soul, of the physical on the psychical? . . . How much allowance, if any, must be made for heredity? How much for environment? For temperament? For sex? . . . The Seelsorger needs to be a lover of this study and an adept in it." [6]

The most Christian of pastors has his difficulties in the application of the gospel to peculiar temperaments and intricate situations. He can easily become content with merely intellectual explanations, delivered to parishioners who are not emotionally ready to receive them, often proving harmful rather than helpful. I remember the unmarried lady in her forties whose mother, with whom she had lived all her life, died at the age of eighty. The daughter was prostrated with grief, became inconsolable, and began to blame God for taking her mother away. All my exhortations to be grateful to God for sparing her mother so many years, and all my declarations concerning the gospel of immortality in Christ only seemed to make her worse. She never came to church again. I believe that if I had been more versed in what has been discovered by careful studies in this field, I might have been more effective in the use of the gospel. It may be that she unconsciously resented the fact that she had had to take care of her mother so many years, at the cost of giving up marriage. Yet she also loved her mother, and the conflict, down deep, gave her a sense of guilt which she transferred to God, thinking consciously only of the fact of death. Psychology has underlined the scriptural statement, "The heart is deceitful above all things." Jesus, we read, "knew what was *in* man."

Although I am not an expert in this field, it seems to me that certain valuable findings of "dynamic" psychology are of the most practical help to pastors in their counseling. As indicated in the previous lecture, they center around the discovery of the importance of the emotions when complicated by unconscious conflicts within the human heart. If these conflicts are conscious, and if a person has a set of values so that he is willing and able to renounce one of the two contradictory issues and to assume responsibility for his decision (Horney), then the situation is very simple. But when he hangs on to his conflict because unconsciously he wants to "eat his cake and have it too," then he must first become aware of the contradictory factors. Let us consider some psychological facts.

1. *Distortions*

Forgetting, it has been found, is often willful. (What would a lover think if his beloved forgot a tryst?) But what people don't want to remember about their attitudes toward others has a way of coming out in their dreams, or in forms of distorted thinking. In Dr. Karl Menninger's terms, some of them are the following: [7]

Projection. A person criticizes others for faults which are really his own. One of the biblical examples is Ahab, the plague of the people of God, who addressed *Elijah* as the one "that troubleth Israel." He probably really thought so. Another is the Hebrew race, in Romans 2: "Wherein thou judgest another, thou condemnest thyself; for thou that judgest doest the same things."

Introjection. Instead of unconsciously palming off our faults on someone else, we may award ourselves another's virtues, or even his faults, like identifying ourselves with actors on the stage. In the extreme form of insanity, the self-identification with Napoleon or Caesar has become a reality to the thinker, so deeply have his inner conflicts driven him from actuality in his flight from himself. In our counseling we may be confronted with someone whose thinking is blocked because every act and purpose is an unconscious mechanical imitation of his father, arising from a hidden guilt feeling at some resentment toward one whom he yet loved and admired.

Displacement. This is the disguising of an unconscious fear or hatred of someone by substituting a different person or thing as the object of the emotion. It happens when a man represses his anger toward his employer at the office and unconsciously takes it out on his wife and children at home. Pastors sometimes find it in those who are bitter and critical of the church, or occasionally in a domineering church councilman frustrated in his daily work or private life.

Rationalization. One of the commonest disguises of unresolved inner conflict is explaining away the real trouble plausibly, but contrarily to the genuine reason for it, conveniently forgetting the whole truth. Thus Adam rationalized his eating of the fruit in addition to projecting his guilt upon Eve. Sometimes when people come to us for counseling, all that they desire is approval of their rationalization or the supply of it. A stingy man has many ways of easing his conscience (quite convincingly to himself) by a logical argument against foreign missions.

Compensation. Closely allied to rationalization, this is the employment of defense mechanisms to protect pride when an unconscious humiliation or inferiority feeling is attacking it. Belligerency may cover a hidden feeling of insecurity. Excessive cleanliness may be a result of unclean sexual habits. Generosity may arise from a fear of not being loved, just as piousness may be an escape for meanness.

These unconscious lies make it impossible for a person to think straight. Sometimes they have so taken hold of all of a life, including the mind, that intellectual arguments or exhortations are not only useless but aggravating.

2. *Unseen Influences*

The theory to account for these disturbances of human life was formulated by Freud. He imagined the soul as composed of three elements: the ego, the superego, and the id. The ego is the conscious life. The superego is the conscience. The id is the unconscious source of instinctive energy, called libido which, to Freud, is entirely sexual, although he and his followers broadened the term so as to make it practically mean "social." The libido, however, seeks pleasure first of all and therefore has within itself a conflict further complicated by a destructive instinct sometimes turned inward. This primal urge, lying entirely in the unconscious, comes to battle with the superego which is composed of conscious or unconscious taboos residing in the mind as a result of training and experience. The ego is the weak and helpless victim or battlefield of the clash between the libido and the superego. The surrounding society and culture join in the fray. When the ego gives up and represses the conflict by forgetfulness, the flight goes on in the unconscious id, like a pent-up fury, all the wilder for being hidden, and breaks out in distortions, anxieties, hostilities, neuroses, panic, fear, and fatigue. Freud's cure was, by hypnotism or free association, to bring to agonizing consciousness the hidden conflict and then to give the driving libido an avenue of release by using it in constructive efforts like social welfare, art, and science. This he called sublimation. It should be carefully noted that Freud did not advocate the unlimited expression of the libido. To him, conscious *suppression* was not harmful as long as the libido was sublimated. What causes trouble is not suppression but *repression,* which is unconscious.

Although Freud held out some hope for mankind through psychoanalysis, he was essentially an atheistic and sex-exaggerating pessimist, and his philosophy has touched many of his craft. Some of his great followers have repudiated his philosophy and corrected his aberrations. His studies and discoveries remain the basis of modern dynamic psychology and cannot be thrust aside by ridicule. Some of their emphases seem to me especially important for the pastor and are herewith noted briefly.

The influence of infanthood upon later life. It has been found that many disturbances of the mind and soul are rooted in infant experiences, especially the love for one parent rather than the other, the cruel harshness of some upbringing, and jealousy of an older or younger brother or sister. Much adult travail of soul may also be caused by a desire to return to infant days, to be a clinging vine, and to crave excessively the affection of others. Every psychological study seems to push back further and further the age when formative influences on later life have their beginning. The Christian emphasis on religious education and home training has, it seems to me, been psychologically vindicated although it never needed to be. But the pastor, by his attention to this development, can be of much greater comfort and help to both parents and children in his parish. Worship, prayer, and love can never begin too early. Jesus and little children are at home together indeed. The family has a social importance never before so vividly realized.

Interpersonal relations are at the heart of mental happiness or misery. It has been discovered that neuroses and other nervous disturbances are seldom caused by calamities, accidents, and difficulties, but almost always by trouble between people which, of course, may sometimes be brought out by crises. Father and daughter, mother and son, husband and wife, brother and sister, lover and beloved, teacher and student, the eternal triangle, employer and employee, and so on, form the breeding place for inner conflicts or the setting for peace. How important become the things that the gospel has always emphasized: love, truth, and the communion of saints.

The importance of sex. Freud's peculiar exaggeration of this element has done harm, but the probability is that as pastors we have not taken it seriously enough. When St. Paul made a list of sins, he always put sexual sins first. I do not mean that the pastor should give sexual instruction. That is something mostly for the home, and (in cases of marital counseling) for the Christian doctor. But the pastor must take into sufficient account the temptations and tensions of people in this area of their life and guard the healthy purity of his own life.

Ambivalence. This awkward word points to a clinically discovered truth: that it is possible to love and hate a person at the same time. When this is frankly faced and resolved in Christian fashion it does no harm. But when allowed to rankle and fight suppressed below the line of consciousness it produces (especially in adolescents) keen anguish.

The effect of the body on the mind. This has been realized throughout human history, as well as its reverse; but modern psychological studies have revealed its power to such an extent that the ancient classical idea of the four humors, one of which dominates every man, is coming back again. At least, it seems to be established that personality is given its general (and more or less unchangeable) cast by bodily birth. Even the new man in Christ Jesus is *that kind* of new man. The benefit of this discovery is that we shall cease to make feverish efforts to change people (including our children) into other persons. Its manifest danger is that we shall blame all our faults on our glands, take a materialistic view of human life, and underrate the power of the gospel to make the same person a new spiritual being: the same person indeed and yet the image of Christ.

These are emphases of the psychology of the unconscious which have helped me in pastoral counseling. To sum them up: as a man thinketh in his heart so is he. As a Christian psychiatrist, to whom I had the good fortune to be able to refer people in my pastorate, once said, "You are not what you think you are. You are what you think: that's what you are!" And in the words of Dr. William S. Sadler, "To tempt the sufferer into confessing what he did not know enough to confess, is the substance of psychiatry."[8] That immediately brings us to the crucial question of guilt and guilt feelings, wherein the greatest help and also the greatest dangers lie for pastors in their use of psychology.

Before we take up that subject, let this important footnote from the writings of Prof. Gordon W. Allport be added to all the above observations: "The bulk of personal motives and traits which comprise the individual are not, as psychoanalysis claims, necessarily rooted in the unconscious. They cannot all be understood simply by deep-sea diving. Conscious motives and manifest behavior are of as great significance as are repressed motives and latent dispositions."[9] And in Christ we are not at the mercy of the devil within us.

3. *Guilt and guilt feelings*

It seems fairly well established that every neurosis has a moral root. And yet at the same time every afflicted person is really a sick person, hardly able to help himself, the victim of evil forces. Unless both of these truths are taken into account, there is no chance of a real and lasting cure. But psychology, as a pure science, can take into account only the second and therefore by itself is impotent. The Christian pastor, and indeed the successful psychiatrist too, must know that in the deep-lying distresses of the human mind, in its unconscious conflicts, there is something to repent of and be absolved of, as well as something to be relieved of.

Take for instance the kinds of distorted thinking described above and consider in their connection the following discerning thoughts of Dr. Karl Heim.[10]

> I know my true nature only when I inspect the impulses which appear quite involuntarily before any ethical reflection can occur. . . . If I hear that my ancient business rival and competitor has had an auto accident and is lying seriously injured in the hospital, my first emotion is malicious joy. . . . A talented young man, who has again and again put me into the shade with his success, achieves a position through his accomplishments, which makes him world famous overnight. The first emotion I feel on hearing the news, is envy. Then moral education comes into play. The question now arises: Since it is not a matter of a conscious decision of will, can we disclaim responsibility for these sordid emotions of malicious joy, envy, hatred and rage? Are we guiltless in the matter? Do we stand in exactly the same relation to them as to an illness or physical pain, which overtakes us without our participation, so that we have nothing for which to reproach ourselves? Surely we cannot go so far. On the contrary, I am even more ashamed of these entirely instinctive and involuntary emotions of vulgar business and professional jealousy, of unconcealed, almost sadistic malicious joy at the misery of a fellow-man, which sweep over me in my first unguarded moments, than of the wrong decisions which I make after careful reflection. I am shocked at the abysmal sordidness, which reveals itself in these impulsive emotions, of which I had not thought myself capable. But I cannot accept with indifference these black emotions, under whose power I am, simply as my fate. I know only too well that they are the very impulses of my heart. I feel myself polluted by them.
>
> The consciousness of guilt is something much more inclusive and incomprehensible than we used to think. Below all, is the feeling of guilt which pertains to the nocturnal depths of our

being, and rises to the level of ordinary consciousness only on special occasions. This guilt lies in our instinctive impulses and emotions, which roll in us like a dark subterranean river.

Guilt situations. Let us take some examples of guilt situations that come to a pastor as counselor.

Miss Emily Jones came to the pastor and said that she stole money from her employer and asked that she be put in prison. She was a good, faithful member of the church. An investigation proved that she did not steal money at all. She had become insane. There was no use telling her she was not guilty. Yet the pastor visited her with the Word of God and brought her at the regular seasons the Sacrament of the Altar for the forgiveness of her sins the same as he did for other sick people. Such occasions aroused no unusual symptoms. I believe they were necessary for her soul. She eventually recovered from her insanity.

Sam Jones came to the pastor because he had committed fornication. He was stricken with guilt and also troubled as to his future attitude toward the girl. It was all out in the open in his mind. There were no hidden elements. He had been a healthy-minded member of the church from his baptism. He had committed a grievous sin. His nature and all his religious training had made the whole thing repulsive. Here again is a simple siutation, one which clearly calls for prayer, declaration of penitence, absolution, and a plan of action by God's strength to overcome the social complications.

John Andrews works in a factory. He daydreams, gets into accidents, and will not associate with his fellow workers. He comes to the pastor with a question about the Bible. As the pastor listens, it is discovered that the boy was brought up with a very narrow and puritanical discipline, and that his trouble is not really with the Bible but with hidden hate against a tyrannical father, now dead, whom he nevertheless had respected and loved.

The first thing is to get that resentment out into the open. The pastor needs to listen and draw out. Even here, however, there is need for a follow-up, for instruction concerning the nature of the Bible, for repentance over a certain amount of willful antipathy toward his father, and for letting it get beyond control. Since the very term "Father" had caused unconscious antagonism and guilt feelings even in church services he needs re-education and a right relation with God through Jesus Christ the Saviour.

Ralph Edwards had trouble with his wife. There was unbearable tension. Both were trying hard to keep the tension from breaking up their marriage. Pastoral counseling of a direct nature did not seem to make any difference. A talk with Ralph alone revealed that he had been brought up to regard sex as unclean, and that he had finally looked upon the marriage act as a sin.

What cured him was a study of God's Word concerning the holy estate of matrimony and the marriage act, and a reminder of the great doctrine that even above conscience stands the Word.

Inez Miller, whose history is so well described by Sherrill, was the third of a family of seven children. Each of the first three had a different father, and Inez' mother had not been married to any of the three men. Resentment at her own discovered illegitimacy, the drunkenness of her stepfather, the invalidism from disease of her mother, the necessity of stopping school in order to work, two unfortunate marriages, and now the trouble with her own neurotic child, all worked together to bring Inez into a mental state where, as usual, guilt feelings predominated. "Who, now," asks Sherrill, "is responsible for what in this tangled web of circumstances?"[11] No doubt this girl "must work out her solution in the realm of feeling," and be relieved of needless, exaggerated, and neurotic guilt feelings. But is that all? Is there not still the need, if she is to build a new life and find her way, for the blessed understanding expressed in the creeds (whose use Sherrill despises), that human sin is deeper than any one known sin, and that as Luther's first thesis states, the whole life of the Christian should be repentance, each day turning to the loving light of the gospel for reassurance and help?

It is significant that our liturgy in the Order for Public Confession has anticipated many of the findings of modern psychology, and yet shown the necessity of confession and absolution, when it provides the prayer, "O God, our Heavenly Father, I confess unto Thee that I have grievously sinned against Thee in many ways; *not only by outward transgression, but also by secret thoughts and desires, which I cannot fully understand, but which are all known unto Thee.*"

It is only by a realization of an absolution that touches these depths, and is even deeper than they are, that a troubled heart is led to get them out into the open. Of this psychology knows nothing.

"PSYCHOLOGIZING" SIN

Pure scientific psychology must exclude such concepts as sin, responsibility, and atonement. Dr. Karl Menninger writes: [12]

> What science or scientist is interested in "justice"? Is pneumonia

just? Or cancer? Or gravity? Or the expansion of steam? What criteria of "justice" can be applied to a broken arm or a weak mind? And to what good end? The scientist is seeking the amelioration of an unhappy situation. This can be secured only if the scientific laws controlling the situation can be discovered and complied with, and not by . . . concepts of equity based on primitive theology. This brings up the conception of "responsibility" with which the psychiatrist is often faced, but with which also he is unconcerned. He has no idea what it means, although he is constantly asked to testify concerning it. The psychiatrist asks not "Is that man responsible?" but "Of what is he capable or incapable?"

One of the best expositions of this limitation of psychology to its own hurt can be found in Hocking's brilliant chapter on "Psychology and the Cure of Souls." [13]

Confession is an acknowledgment of sin; (psycho)analysis is a discovery of mistake or misfortune. Confession involves penitence; analysis brings escape from penitence. Confession remains morally difficult and does not emerge into an atmosphere . . . of scientific interest.

To the psychologist there is no such thing as a good or bad person, only a fortunate or unfortunate one. But this will satisfy the inner need of no one, because his need is always at bottom moral and religious.

Confession is an acknowledgment of sin; (psycho)analysis is a judgment. . . . If science is a partial judge of life, if science in omitting the moral ingredient, omits an essential part of true judgment, then confession to the scientist must by its own logic be incomplete. . . . The valid confessor must stand *in loco Dei*. . . . The rankling center of mental disease is that one strives to cloak from himself what he cannot conceal from the universe: it is *that* pocket which must be lanced.

Yet the most popular recent books on pastoral counseling have fallen into the snare. According to Wise,[14]

> The approach we are outlining here will create conflicts in ministers holding the traditional attitude. The question often comes, "Must we never pass judgment?" It is good psychology to answer this question in the negative. . . . The counselor does not pronounce forgiveness nor does he give people forgiveness. . . . The grace of God lies in the real fact that He has created within human personality powers which, if properly used, will result in the healing of personality and a more creative way of life . . . through the process of acceptance, clarification, and release. . . . There is a curative, creative, redemptive force inherent in man.

Dicks writes,[15]

> The old heaven and hell have passed away and the old-fashioned authority of the clergyman with them. . . . (For a parishioner) to participate in the creative role (of God), . . . is to have gained the kingdom of heaven already—perhaps one should say, released the kingdom of heaven within us—while to fail to develop one's capacities . . . is to accept hell. . . . There is one further thought in this connection that influences our pastoral work: the nature of Christ's death is of relatively little importance so far as the pastor's work is concerned.

Here is a sad and complete capitulation of the gospel of Christ and his atonement to the restrictive dogmas of psychologism. One hesitates to believe that down in their hearts these Christian writers realize where their theologizing leads them.

Two things seem to have swept them into the shallows. The first is a reaction against ministers who are moralistic and pompous, a reaction made the more violent by the discoveries of the right use of nondirective counseling as a listening technique. As Hocking puts it, "The moral element of judgment may be so far censorious as to inhibit the beginnings of confession, and this may be the temperamental disqualification of the Protestant clergy as a class as hearers of confession."

The second is more serious: a liberalistic neglect of the

effective application to psychology of the Reformation emphasis upon the distinction between law and gospel, and between justification and sanctification. "God sent not his Son into the world to condemn the world, but that the world through him might be saved." The gospel must be predominant, and no true Christian pastor can be a moralistic and legalistic tyrant. Yet the law is divine and necessary as the schoolmaster to bring us to Christ. The subject will be further considered in connection with preaching.

JUSTIFICATION AND SANCTIFICATION

Justification is God for us. Sanctification is God within us. Both are necessary. But before God can be felt as within us, he must be felt as for us. The pastoral counseling movement, in rejecting the first thereby vitiates the second, upon which nevertheless it bases everything.

What is most deeply needed by any person in mental or spiritual trouble is not *first of all* the feeling that God is within him, but first of all the feeling that God is for him in Christ even in his worst condition and in his deepest guilt. He needs something as a start, which goes back of his own distressing lack of moral and spiritual power, something deeper than any claim upon his mind by the id or the superego or libido or hidden influences of childhood or any other principalities and powers, something far greater than anything he can ever find in himself. In a word, he must have faith in the gospel of the atonement, and that faith must be given to him through the Word.

The neglect of this important fact is found, for instance, in Boisen's frank book. In his dealing with souls, he says, he tries to bring the person " . . . restoration to the fellowship of that social something which we call God, . . . to get him to see that . . . he is worthy of honor in so far as he is earnestly seeking to become better. That, as I understand it, is what Paul meant when he talked about faith as against works." [16] But "earnestly seeking to become better" is exactly what the stricken person often does not have the power to do. It is his central trouble. As Otto A. Piper points out, "Where faith is interpreted in a purely psychological sense and the divine initiative in its genesis is ignored, faith seems to bring about a gradual approximation to God. . . . The communion with God which the believer enjoys has been made possible by justification. It does not rest upon some divine element or faculty which supposedly belongs to man's nature but rather upon that new worthiness of a child of God in Jesus Christ, which God by His grace grants to the believer." [17] In other words, somehow the Word must be present, even in the earliest stages of a person's difficulties. A forgiving act of God (justification) must precede in some way the soul's use of the power of God to become better. Here lies the real skill of the pastoral counselor, and here opens a field of investigation that has not even been entered by the modern pastoral counseling movement. For this movement has practically thrown out of the pastoral counseling act the elements of revelation, judgment, atonement, and the divine initiative. Sometimes there has consequently been an entire surrender to the psychological axiom that the aim of treatment has nothing to do with the removal of guilt, but only with the relief of guilt *feelings,* and that salvation is exactly equivalent to a *feeling* of health and calm (such as David had before Nathan spoke to him).

Dr. Dicks seems even to think that this is "Protestantism." He says,[18]

> Reassurance, for the Protestant, is what the statement of absolution is for the Catholic, psychologically. "I absolve you in the name of the Father and the Son and the Holy Ghost," is the Catholic statement following confession. The statement of reassurance (of the Protestant) is, "I believe you will be all right"; "I can see a lot of hope in your case"; "I have faith this will not throw you"; "There is no such thing as being ruined except as you think you are, and you don't think so in this case"; "I believe in you and I'm going to see you through." A soul-companion never condemns, never judges, but always attempts to aid. You will note in the above statements of reassurance that the Catholic absolution is pronounced in the name of the Trinity, while the Protestant reassurance is pronounced in the name of the pastor and personalized around him. This is an advantage in that it is intimate and personal; it is a disadvantage in that it is human and thought of as human by the parishioner. The Protestant's reassurance is limited in that it lacks perspective, the far view, the support of the Creator Himself.

Dr. Dicks presumes to speak for Protestants but he is certainly not speaking for Lutherans.

Far more dangerous and frightening than the unconscious, the id, the libido, and the clash with the superego, is the willful rebellion of sin against God that lies in all of us. And far more powerful than even the useful techniques of pure scientific psychology are the gospel, the Word, Christ, the atonement, and the Holy Spirit.

Christianity can use the blessings of proved psychological discoveries, but it can never be the handmaiden of its limited therapies. As a matter of fact, most people are more worried about their troubles than about their sins. If they can get rid of their troubles without getting rid of their sins, they are more than satisfied. *And these are precisely the people who finally throng the psychiatrist's office and prove to be his worst problems.*

SUMMARY

How much psychology, then, should a pastor know? In a word, all he possibly can. Not in a way to make him morbid, or to neglect the other fields of knowledge which his ministry requires even more, or to become intoxicated by claims of an infant science, or to let his approach to people be imprisoned and stifled by pure secularism—but enough to teach him how to seek out the inner motives of men, to sympathize with the plight of those caught in the net of their hidden conflicts, and to help his parishioners to bring out and face the truth about themselves. Let the gospel occupy the throne.

III

WHAT SHALL I TELL PEOPLE?

I will bless the Lord, who hath given me counsel.

PSALM 16:7

I have not shunned to declare unto you all the counsel of God.

ACTS 20:27

"Tell the people!" said God to Isaiah. And Paul, the elder pastor wrote to Timothy, the younger one, "If thou put the brethren in remembrance of these things, thou shalt be a good minister of Jesus Christ, nourished up in the words of faith and of good doctrine. . . . Reprove, rebuke, exhort with all longsuffering and doctrine." Yet he also says, "Rebuke not an elder, but intreat him as a father; and the younger men as brethren; the elder women as mothers; the younger as sisters, with all purity." That is apostolic pastoral counseling.

Pastors talk too much? Without doubt! There are times when the pastor must be quiet and say nothing, and when he must be careful not to interfere with the process whereby a parishioner unburdens himself. This is the great truth of the present pastoral counseling movement. Its studies have shown us how skillful the pastor needs to be in order to further by sympathetic listening and clarification the parishioner's gradual facing of himself, allowing the consequent decisions to be entirely the parishioner's own.

To restrict pastoral counseling to this one phase seems to me, however, impossible and self-defeating when attempted.

The parishioner must indeed become independent of the pastor but he still needs God and he still needs guidance. As I have tried to show previously, God is needed not only in pre-counseling and post-counseling, but during the process of insight itself. And to say that God is needed is to say that his revelation, his Word, his gospel is needed. Again the pastor's skill is called for, as well as his understanding that the gospel is not just good advice or rules, or information.

When people come to a Christian pastor, they expect him to "know what is in man." But they also expect him to know what is *not* in them, and what could never be gotten out of themselves alone: the mercy of a holy and just God. The Christian pastor has a calling, not merely to make his people feel responsible for themselves but find fellowship with the One who has revealed himself in Christ.

God has spoken, in his Word, about his regard for the children of men when they are in difficulties. I propose to consider his counsels for situations of sickness, loneliness, marriage problems, and the anxieties of parents for their children. There are many others. Let these suffice, leaving certain further questions to the next lecture.

THE SICK

The organically ill

"The everlasting mercy," is the chief need of sick people. They are at the mercy of everybody and everything: the doctor, the nurses, the hospital and its strange routine, the family situation, the work back at the office, pain, money, and visitors. The ordinary props have been knocked out from under them. The future is insecure. They are often perplexed, baffled, frightened, and sometimes bitter and fretful. To have a trusted pastor to whom they can talk is a great relief in itself, but there is still the necessity of an eternal Refuge. Their dependency is a total picture, and includes pangs of conscience or regret. It needs the everlasting arms.

Here is where Scripture and prayer work their power strikingly. The eighth chapter of Romans, I have found to work miracles. "If God be for us, who can be against us? He that spared not his own Son, but delivered him up for us all, how shall he not with him also freely give us all things? . . . Who shall separate us from the love of Christ? shall tribulation, or distress (or sickness)? . . . Nay, in all these things we are more than conquerors through him that loved us. For I am persuaded, that neither death, nor life, nor angels, nor principalities, nor powers, nor things present, nor things to come, nor height, nor depth, nor any other creature, shall be able to separate us from the love of God, which is in Christ Jesus our Lord."

It must be an *everlasting* mercy. It is well for the pastor to point out the clinching "omnibus" words in God's promises: "I will *never* leave thee nor forsake thee. . . . Casting *all* your care upon him, for he careth for you. . . . *Nothing* shall be able to separate us from the love of God. . . . God so loved *the world* that he gave his only begotten Son, that *whosoever* believeth in him should not perish but have everlasting life. . . . *Him* (anyone) that cometh unto me I will *in no wise* cast out. . . . Come unto me, *all* ye that labor and are heavy laden, and I will give you rest. . . . The mercy of the Lord is *everlasting*."

Prayer, I believe, should never be omitted, even if it must

be very brief, only a word or two. In my beginning ministry I prayed only when asked to do so. That lasted two weeks. I found out my mistake. Then for a while I asked the parishioner whether he wished me to pray. That lasted a little longer. Finally I learned to say simply, "I am going to pray with you" and to do it on every visit with almost no exceptions.

Real prayer is not a generalizing soliloquy. It is a two-way conversation with God. That is, it takes hold of a promise which God has declared and lays claim upon it with thanksgiving. It is said that one should never pray for the patient to get well, lest he fail to recover and lose his faith. By that kind of reasoning, nothing should ever be prayed for. The Bible says, "in *every thing* . . . with thanksgiving let your requests be made known unto God. And the peace of God, which passeth all understanding, shall keep your hearts and minds through Christ Jesus." The words, "with thanksgiving" and "through Christ Jesus" are the saving salt. True prayer trusts first in God's mercy and goes on with both submission and hope to "Thy will be done," then makes its petitions known and ends with confidence in Him.

Sick visits should be short. That is part of the mercy we owe our beloved parishioners. Many pastors make it a rule not to sit down. Of course all rules have their exceptions.

The insane

When a parishioner is insane, his sickness calls for the same Christian emphasis as any other illness: the love of God in Christ Jesus. That is both good Christianity and good psychiatry.

The mentally ill have been called the most neglected of all

church people. Pastors are afraid there is nothing they can do, and put them down at the end of their sick lists. This fear is entirely without foundation. As the superintendent of a mental hospital once said, "The mind of an insane person is closed. But sometimes the door opens a little bit, often when we are not aware of it." The pastor's visit may coincide with one of these moments of slight opening, or even cause it. A word may slip in and sink deep: the names of the Heavenly Father and the Divine Mediator, the familiar Creed or Lord's Prayer, and so on. No argument, of course, is in place. In my own experience, visitation with mentally sick parishioners has been most rewarding. It should be remembered in this connection that one half of the hospital beds in America are occupied by mental patients, and that one out of every ten persons now living will need psychiatric care at some time during his life. To neglect such a vast area of human life, in our ministry, would indeed be shameful. It should also be remembered that fully half of the patients who enter a state hospital come out cured.

Chaplain J. Obert Kempson (one of our Lutheran pastors who is now ministering at the State Hospital in Columbia, S. C.), has written an excellent article on this subject in which he quotes Dr. William A. White as saying that the patient's words and actions should be carefully noted, because through them the patient is trying to tell us something. [1] Sometimes the pastor can discover a lead. A mental patient, like any other, often feels isolated, lonely, and strange. It is a great help to him to know that he is not forgotten. Letters, Sunday church bulletins, church school literature, and daily devotional booklets are very welcome, as well as visits and wisely planned gift packages. The pastor must, of course, not become the messenger of all the patient's wishes. But there are many practical things he can do, such as counseling with the patient who fears entrance into a state hospital, visiting his family, and guiding both patient and family when the patient returns home, restoring him also to the companionship of the congregation.

A pastor should be alert to the signs of insanity in his parishioners so as to provide the necessary referral. There seem to be at present three general classifications of functional psychosis: schizophrenia, manic-depressive behavior, and involutional melancholia.

Schizophrenia (dementia praecox), etymologically is "scissor-mindedness." The personality is clipped in two. The man is beside himself. His flight into daydreaming has become so complete that the daydream is a reality to him. His real self is unknown. He lives entirely in another world. He may go into seclusion or stupor, or he may be very glib and talkative. He suddenly does queer things which are meaningful only to himself, he may hear voices, and he often refers to himself in the third person. On the other hand he may become a dangerous paranoiac who believes that he is being constantly persecuted, talked about, and plotted against.

The manic-depressive soul is up one moment and down the next. Sometimes the exalted or depressed period extends for a long time. In the high moments he may suddenly spend extravagantly or talk hysterically. In his low periods he may be in danger of suicide. All people have pendulum motions of this kind to some extent, and manic-depressives frequently recover.

Involutional melancholia is attached to "change of life."

The signs which sometimes betray these sufferings to the pastor in the lives of his parishioners are said to be change of personality, extreme apathy or irritability, illusions, stupor, vagrancy, exaggerated guilt feelings, and entirely senseless actions. The pastor also needs to calm the feeling which normal people often get from misunderstanding or from too much morbid reading: that they are going insane. However, he should never discount an expressed intent to commit suicide.

The neurotic

Much has already been said about those who come for pastoral counseling because of mental and spiritual disturbances which are not insanity at all but whose inner conflicts block normal living. In their serious forms, I believe that the pastor should never attempt cure, but always refer them to a physician. In their milder forms the pastor must do his best with God's help and the patience of the Scriptures. The great need again is for a wise love: kindness and firmness unlimited. Some of these people have their affliction to the end of their lives: imaginary aches and pains (which are nevertheless very real to themselves), exhaustion, and trouble in getting along with people. Some of them make out, not only in spite of their neurosis but occasionally it seems because of it. They are sick. Let the pastor recognize that. They cannot be cured by palliatives, or by callous exhortations to "buck up" and "get your mind off yourself," and "stop worrying." Poor souls, that is just what they cannot do. To say these things makes them worse. No sickness is so terrible. None more deserves our pity and patience. But we must not do them harm by allowing constant daily visits to the parsonage and endless talking. And yet, with their helpless sickness, they are the only ones who can help themselves. Here lies the difficulty, and it calls not only for pity but also for the ministry of the gospel to a responsible soul. They need God's Word and the understanding fellowship of Christians.

Homosexuality and extreme alcoholism are subjects with which every pastor, sooner or later, must deal. But they are shrouded in mystery. Both the homosexual and the extreme alcoholic are sick people, it is true, and need medical attention, although some very high medical authorities declare that they are essentially incurable.

On the other hand, a moral element is undoubtedly present in each of them, for which the pastor must be alert. A homosexual can, with understanding, be made to realize that he must control himself and not glorify his weakness as so many do, even considering themselves the elite of human society. One eminent psychiatrist told me that a smash to the jaw by an intended victim is the best possible treatment.

The same duality is present in the alcoholic. He is sick, and yet he must ultimately cure himself. Self-pity is his worst enemy, and treating him merely as a sick person weakens the moral power for recovery. Indeed, the success of Alcoholics Anonymous is based upon the will to be cured, faith in God, and the help of others who are under the same affliction. The pastor will find here the most baffling of all his attempts at ministry, yet he should never give up.

THE FORSAKEN

The aged, the shut-ins, and the bereaved are a group together who have a special need: *an outlook for the future* and a *sense of usefulness*. Through faith they need to arrive at hope and love. Their discovery of that faith is one of the most inspiring examples for all of us. It is frequently a sermon to the preacher himself. The fellowship of the church reaches out in its most unselfish form of ministry to the forsaken.

The aged

"At eventime, there shall be light." That is a promise which Christian counseling helps bring to pass. By frequent visitation, old people need to bask in the recollection of former days; but they also need news of the world about them, the company of the young, and above all, the familiar passages of Scripture. Some pastors are using tape recordings of church services to bring to them.

An ailing, aged person with clear mind, facing imminent death needs the ministration of the pastor every day or two, that the light of heaven may be kept burning in the midst of their desolation, and sometimes in their panic.

Ministry to the dying is one of the pastor's most solemn responsibilities. The special order for it in the Occasional Service Book is based not only on good theology but also on insight into the need of the soul. The recitation of the majestic words of the Creed, simple and full of the peace that passes understanding, kindles anew the flickering faith.

Nowadays, with people living longer, proper attention is beginning to be given to the bodily and mental complications of old age. A new science is arising, called geriatrics.

Ministry to the aged and dying seems to be a mark of the Lutheran church. Dr. Dicks writes,[2]

> In talking with a Lutheran pastor one day I asked, "For how many of your people are you called when they are dying?" He looked at me with something of wonder at the question. "Why,

> all of them," he said. "What happens when you are out of town?" I asked. He answered, "There is always someone to take the calls, either my assistant or a brother minister. I would no more think of not having my parish covered for emergency calls than a doctor would of going away without arranging for someone to take care of his patients." Contrast this with a situation which came to my attention when a seriously ill patient in a Chicago hospital expressed the desire to see a minister of another denomination and it took three days to even find one, as all had gone off to a conference which had been called by one of the denominational leaders.

I fear Dr. Dicks is over generous to the Lutherans on this point, however.

Shut-ins

"Behold, I have set before thee an open door and no man can shut it." With that assurance, shut-ins need never feel shut-in. God will not let their life become a blind alley or a walled prison. No one is useless while he loves, and no one is useless while someone loves him. These are demonstrable facts, examples of which all pastors can cite. Counseling calls for appropriate action, and the pastor can enlist and train laymen to help him. One of the most curious experiences of my ministry was that I found shut-ins the best source of all the latest news.

The bereaved

One of the best psychological studies of grief is found in the researches of Dr. Erich Lindemann.[3] He lists some of the acute effects: bodily distress, a feeling that things are unreal, idolizing of the departed, frequent feelings of guilt over not having done enough for him, coldness and irritability toward others, inability to carry on the day's work, and sometimes even the taking on of the characteristics and behavior traits of the deceased.

The Bible says that our first Christian duty to bereaved people is to visit them: to visit the fatherless and the widows in their affliction is real religion. They need someone to talk to who loves them. The pastor's calling after the funeral is sometimes as important as his visits before. "They need to talk of their beloved until the idealized image comes nearer to the real one." Fears, bitterness, and discontent need to be poured out, losing much of their strength and sting in the process.

A blessed counsel of God to the bereaved is the promise of God that He has *a continuing and new purpose for them,* no matter how illustrious the departed may have been. The eleventh chapter of Hebrews lists the heroes of the faith. But then it goes on to say, "All these, having attained a good report through faith, received not the promise: God having provided some better thing for us, that they without us should not be made perfect." That is, they did their part and now they are waiting, like a great cloud of witnesses, for us to do our part. Otherwise theirs would not become perfected. "God has a purpose for you." That is what a sorrowing soul needs to realize in its desolation.

Another counsel of God which applies also to all the other catastrophes of life is the glowing word of I Corinthians 10:13: "There hath no trial taken you but such as is common to man: but God is faithful, who will not let you be tried above that ye are able; but will with the trial also make a way to escape, that ye may be able to bear it" (not run away from it). It is quite proper to put the word "trial" in place of "temptation" in this verse, since that is the way the original is frequently translated, and the biblical English also has the double meaning. The point is that people sometimes get the fixed idea that God "has it in for them," that they have done something special to be punished for, and that even though they have tried to be good the evil prosper and there is no meaning to things. (They have never read Job.) Losing their moral moorings, fear grips them: fear of the past or of the unconscious or of people, and finally of God. A prayer of thanksgiving for their blessings which are far above merit, incorporating the great promise of I Corinthians 10:13, will help to lift their souls to safety again. In all, the forgiveness of God in Christ must be central. Then the thoughts of resurrection, immortality, reunion, and heaven can mean something.

MARRIAGE

Marriages ought to be saved, and usually can be. Whether the pastor will put much work on saving them depends upon whether he believes God's Word about marriage. In spite of the failures that every pastor experiences, the field is fruitful, helpful, and hopeful, because of the rich counsels of Christ.

"He which made them in the beginning. . ." Jesus, in treating of marriage and divorce, went right back to creation. His pointed words concerning one husband and one wife were uttered, he said, not because he had something new to tell; it was "from the beginning." Monogamy is rooted, not in superstitious taboo or arbitrary rule, but in creation itself. It is natural for one man to have one woman. It is not just a requirement of advanced civilization. When two people look upon marriage in this exalted way it gives them a feeling that

all their quarrels and disagreements are worth struggling with for the sake of creation itself — for the divine order of things. The pastor, furthermore, knows that all the powers of creation are back of him in his efforts to save a threatened home.

"... *made them male and female* ..." Sex is honorable, not unclean. Sexual abstinence can be unclean, not holy. St. Paul said, "Defraud ye not one the other, except it be with consent for a time . . . and come together again, that Satan tempt you not for your incontinency." Birth control, if it be for the purpose of preferring comforts or pleasure to the raising of a family of children, is against the Creator's command and the course of nature.

". . . *and said, For this cause shall a man leave father and mother* . . .". It is frequently the in-laws and other relatives that cause trouble in marriage, very often because an astonishing number of young men and young women believe that the parent-child relationship is closer than that of husband and wife. The tie of marriage is recognized by both the Bible and the state as the closest of all. Even a couple's love for their children should not come before their love for each other. When a woman marries she leaves father and mother and she and her relatives must know in all Christian courtesy and patience that this is so.

". . . *and cleave to his wife* . . ." Women need love and affection perhaps even more than men, and a husband makes a serious mistake when he fails to tell his wife every day that he loves her. Men need it too. Love requires demonstration. And it needs cultivation, nourishment, attention, respect, and even will power. A great Christian once testified to me his belief that love is fifty per cent will power. Countless are the influences of society today, in time, interest, and temptation, whose effect is to break up love. In fact, if romantic attachment were the essence of marriage, as some seem to think it is, then the home could never stand.

"*. . . and they twain shall be one flesh . . .*" It is miraculous how husband and wife become one, as the years go on. Patience, mutual understanding, forbearance, absolute honesty, and good will, settle most of the problems of marriage, even the sexual ones; and the mutual delight in each other grows richer with time. God's power is always at work.

"*What therefore God hath joined together, let not man put asunder.*" The religious sanction of marriage, and the common church life together, are strong foundations. Where the two pledge their troth not only to each other, but to God, there is a divine triangle that destroys any possibility of the other kind of triangle. When love to each other grows weak, the tie with God keeps it from falling apart. If love to God grows weak, love for each other strengthens it.

The church can do much by marital counseling. It can do much more by upholding the religious nature of marriage and refusing to lend its office and blessing to divorce except on the biblical grounds of adultery or malicious desertion. Counseling should include these Christian sanctions.

"*The husband is the head of the wife.*" Paul's words did not give the husband one inch of advantage over the wife, as a careful study of his teachings will show, but they do indicate that there ought to be order in the home. There has to be a head of the house. Money causes much marital distress where Paul's words would help. In his writings, for each prerogative of the husband he presents a corresponding honor for the wife which makes exploitation, tyranny, selfishness, and unfairness an impossibility. He establishes partnership for both.

If there is some religious feeling in the individuals involved, no case of marital trouble is hopeless. I had that impressed on me by one of the most complicated of situations. Jim and Sarah had both been divorced before. He came to me in great distress when she ran away. I had to go after her, with him, and bring her back. Each of them had been a church member, but she of another denomination and he a lapsed member of my own church. I had scenes with them thereafter when he tore down the curtains in a rage and threw crockery around the room. She had been going around with another man. When I went after her another time, her parents sheltered her and I had to tell them the truth about her and bring her back. I got both of them to an excellent psychiatrist, who tried hard and finally called them worthless. Yet deep down in each of them was some religion; otherwise they wouldn't have kept coming to me. I counseled them separately and together, listening to sordid details. I found that the Bible meant something to them and I therefore used frequently the passages on forgiveness. By the grace of God, in spite of all the varied obstacles against the success of that marriage, it lasted through the years to their mutual happiness until the day of his death. It taught me never to give up as long as a spark of religion remained or could be kindled. It made up for many of my failures.

The power of church life together is, I think, testified to by the records of one particular congregation over a period of twenty-five years. They show that whenever two members of the congregation were married by the pastor of the church (whoever he was), there was never serious trouble.

PARENTS AND CHILDREN

I used to give advice to parents on how to bring up their children. Then I had three of my own. Now I don't give advice any more. I know now that all children are different, even in the same family, and that there is no general formula. Even the Bible does not give a formula, although it has valuable counsel for the heart. What does one do when Johnnie is incorrigible? When are the times, if ever, when a child is to be kissed, spanked, or left alone? No pastor, and no psychologist either, can tell parents what to do in every case, or what methods are sacrosanct. One of the most excruciating causes of worry to parents is the indiscriminate chorus of blame which certain schools of psychology have heaped upon the heads of father and mother — especially mother.

Many of my hearers will recall the days of behaviorism, under the leadership of Dr. John R. Watson, who discounted almost completely the power of heredity when measured against that of "conditioned reflexes." Children were to be fed at certain hours no matter how hungry they ever became, nor how loudly they let it be known. Natural functions were to be trained exactly, chronologically, and severely. Above all, any show of affection on the part of the parent was to be suppressed: no kissing, no fondling. I recall a poem that appeared in the *New York Herald Tribune* at the time, headed by a quotation from Dr. Watson reading, "The fact that this mother-love is responsible for a large number of divorces, a larger number of unhappy marriages . . . is not enough to keep mothers from petting their children."

> Oh, little baby that I love,
> I may but kiss your brow;

And what would Dr. Watson say
If he could see us now!

Oh, little baby, dear and fair,
Why were you made so small,
If I was not to cuddle you
Or snuggle you at all?

But little children all should be
Dispassionately wise,
And look at "mother-love" with cool
And disapproving eyes.

Then life will grow so rational
(Not silly, as before)
That we shall be too wise to have
These babies any more.

Today the swing of the pendulum is far in the other direction. It is now claimed that many divorces and unhappy marriages, and much of the crime and callousness of the day, are the direct results of parents' not showing affection to their children, who grow up without a feeling of security, and are therefore plagued by inner conflicts and emotional disturbances. They felt rejected in their youth, and today hostility and anxiety are the result.

Many will remember, also, the day of "expressionism" which still persists but in much corrected form. The general idea was to let the child do what he would, lest he become a frustrated being.

Today the emphasis on the need of love toward children has sometimes been presented in such form that it frightens fathers and mothers away from any discipline or guidance at all. The fear of the effect of childhood experiences upon the unconscious has caused such lack of any real leadership of youth, that the best psychologists of our day are now warning parents it is just as bad to leave a child upon his own as it is to love him too little. Common sense, as always, is invoked by the best child experts, and is reflected in the cartoon of the precocious small boy saying to his thwarted frowning parents: "And remember that years from now I'll probably be telling everything you say to a psychiatrist." Another shows an irate father looking at a youngster who has deliberately snatched the cover off the table to let the lamp crash in broken pieces on the floor. The mother is quoting to the father from an open book in her hand, "This book says he does that because he feels nobody loves him. Now go and show him you do."

The one great truth emerging nevertheless out of all these shifts in theory is the importance of the influences upon later life of the experiences of infanthood and early childhood. Coupled with this is the truth that much of a parent's difficulty with children arises out of the unconscious experiences of his own early youth and upbringing. It is enough to frighten good parents out of their wits, and perhaps frighten bad parents into becoming better ones.

There are in God's Word three emphases which support the findings of the scientists and which bring divine comfort and guidance.

(1) *You can't respect your children too much.* "Let the little children come unto me," said Jesus, "for of such is the kingdom of heaven." We spend our time trying to get children to behave like adults. Jesus puts the emphasis on the other side. "Except ye become as little children, ye shall not enter into the kingdom of heaven." They are precious souls before God, each with his individuality. Children should not be

treated as toys, playthings, and means for amusement. They have capacities and possibilities we do not dream of. "We are born originals, we die copies," is the sad commentary on much child training. All this is quite different from idolizing children which springs not from respecting them but from satisfying one's own emotions and pride. To press children beyond their capacity, forcing them into moulds and skills they do not possess, is again not respecting but disrespecting them. Every child has a direct responsibility to God, which should be nurtured in respect to his age, by training in prayer, repentance, forgiveness, and joy in the baptismal covenant.

(2) *You can't love your children too much.* Real love of children will never spoil them. A parent who spoils a child loves himself, not the child. The cure of an unwise love is more love, not less. Our model here is God himself, whose representatives we are. As a father, says the Bible, he chastens but always in love. "He that spareth the rod hateth his son." And coupled with the adjuration, "Children, obey your parents in all things: for this is well pleasing unto the Lord," is the admonition to parents: "Provoke not your children to anger, lest they be discouraged; but bring them up in the nurture and admonition of the Lord." Psychologists have shown, indeed, how hard it is for a parent to love a child if the parent hates himself because of hidden moral conflicts within his breast, or if he is suffering under forgotten shocks of his own childhood. Psychology has not sufficiently investigated the power of the gospel to resolve these inner conflicts and to provoke a Christian love that, for Christ's sake, counteracts their bad influence.

(3) *You cannot have too much patience.* No Bible reader can escape the emphasis upon the grace of patience in every

hope of the Christian life. One whole book (Hebrews) is devoted to it. It is one of the prime virtues of the parent, and as necessary as the air he breathes.

"Patience" is a popularly misunderstood word. It seems to mean sitting still and doing nothing. That is not patience, but apathy. Patience is a rich word composed of several elements.

One of these elements is endurance. "Endure hardness, as a good soldier of Jesus Christ." Parents' troubles are often solved just by "taking it" and waiting. It means not fainting. Parents are sometimes like men in a hurricane: they just have to hold on. Many things right themselves in time. The storm blows over. The patient person will not give in to panic or rashness or wrong means to a difficult good end.

Another element of patience is persistence. "Ask, and it shall be given you; seek, and ye shall find; knock, and it shall be opened unto you," said Jesus, speaking of importunate and persistent prayer. A good thing is worth keeping after. In the growing life of children, patience means repeated and unflagging repetition which is the price of knowledge and of many other riches. When the foolishness of a certain pursuit reveals itself, the chase should be abandoned. But no good quality of character, and no accomplishment of good influence, were ever won in the first skirmish.

The most important ingredient of patience is confidence! It is based upon the Christian parent's conviction that in giving him children, God has shown his trust in him and that therefore he can trust God in turn for all the wisdom, strength, and love he needs for his sacred task. After all (a parent must remind himself), Christ loves these children of mine even more than I do. About all a parent can do, when in a quandary, is to lift his eyes in a prayer of partnership, and say, "O God, I'll do my very best right to the limit, but the rest is up to You!" God has a purpose for these children of ours even independently of (and sometimes in spite of) our own efforts. We can trust him!

SUMMARY

There are exceedingly few occasions when a pastor ought to give advice to his parishioners. He ought to lead them to make their own decisions. He ought never to talk too much, and when hidden emotional conflicts seem to be the cause of trouble he ought to give uninterrupted *and uninhibited* opportunity for their release. But he withholds from them his greatest treasure if somewhere *in every total situation* he fails to strengthen the Christian framework of their problem, or fails to feed their faith with the revealed Word of God. Toward this skill, psychology and the church need jointly to make studies that so far have never been seriously attempted.

IV

WHY DON'T PEOPLE COME TO ME?

There are many devices in a man's heart; nevertheless the counsel of the Lord, that shall stand. PROVERBS 19:21

Let us ask first, "Where *do* people take their troubles?" A few years ago Dr. Lee R. Steiner set out to answer this question, and wrote a book on it under that title.[1] She hung out a shingle and listed herself in the telephone directory under the heading of "Advisory Service." She also represented herself as a troubled soul and investigated the various sources of counseling. Her book is a marvel to read. The number of places where people go is unbelievable.

She gives due respect, of course, to the church and to recognized, approved professions and agencies outside of the church, like the United States Employment Service, the National Vocational Guidance Association, the various marriage counseling services, and governmental organizations on the state and local level. As we all know, there are also three responsible professions that deal with the mind. Psychoanalysts follow exclusively the main Freudian method of deep therapy, the treatment usually covering several visits a week for a year or more. They are M.D.'s. They have had to undergo psychoanalysis themselves, and to take postgraduate training in the method. Psychiatrists are also M.D.'s and depend much upon Freudian theory but also use many other methods, this group being larger in number than that of the psychoanalysts. They form a large section of the staffs of mental hospitals and also engage in private practice. Many neurologists are also trained in psychiatry. Practicing psychologists are not M.D.'s, but have had thorough training in graduate study and are usually Ph.D.'s. They are employed in industry, education, and other fields, or have their own private practice. There are few laws controlling them in most states. It seems that almost anybody can set up his office and advise people for pay. Consequently, this thoroughly respectable profession shades off rapidly into charlatanry.

Dr. Steiner found counselors on newspapers and in magazines, as well as in radio and television. There were also the astrologers, the craniologists, the palmists, the graphologists, the numerologists, the telepathists, the spiritualists, the lonely-heart experts, the success schools, the charm classes, Christian Science, New Thought, Unity, the Oxford Movement, Yoga, Theosophy and the various hotel parlor meetings. Millions of people go to these sources and others like them for counsel. No mention is here made of the host of books and articles giving similar types of advice.

Can we doubt that some of our church people use these sources also? Why do they not come to the pastor?

The pastor will, of course, rejoice that those who go to some of these places for the purpose they have in mind do *not* come to him. Pitiful souls, they want magic answers to take the place of thinking, easy formulas for happiness, short cuts to success, and excuses for doing what they want to do.

The pastor can also be thankful for a minimum of chronic complainers and of those who would use him as a tool. "Who made me a judge or a divider over you?" said Jesus when someone came to him for an easy answer on how to settle an inheritance. "Speak to my brother," he said, and Jesus refused. Sometimes a wife wants the pastor to speak to her husband, or a parent to his boy, when they themselves are the ones who need a change of heart and thought. In like manner Jesus, seeing what was in the man, said to this enquirer, "Take heed, and beware of covetousness: for a man's life consisteth not in the abundance of the things which he possesseth."

In other words, there are good and bad reasons why people do not come to the pastor for counseling. The reason why some do not come may reflect honor rather than blame upon him. No pastor can measure the failure or success of his ministry simply by counting the number of those who come to him.

So important is the individual ministry of the pastor, however, that he will want to check on himself, and ask whether the condition of his own Christian personality may be keeping away from his door the sinful and suffering soul who needs the Word from him.

THE PASTOR'S PERSONALITY

Why don't people come to me? Perhaps I'm harsh, dogmatic, talkative, and censorious. Or maybe on the other hand I'm flippant, sentimental, and shallow. Perhaps it's because I deal with ideas more than with people, and have no real sympathy and concern. Or is it because I am more interested in increasing the membership statistics, raising the budget, or attending conferences? Is my manner too cold and forbidding, or too effusive and anxious?

Recently I looked over the 427 names of pastors in our synod for a certain year about a decade ago. Thirty-nine of them had serious difficulty, centering on their trouble in getting along with others. Of the thirty-nine, seventeen had trouble with their own inner make-up, although they did not realize it at the time. Of the others, ten had troubles with their wives, in some cases by their own fault but by no means in all; six had neurotic trends, five were sex offenders, and one was an alcoholic. Of the seventeen with inner difficulties, one had trouble with his temper, another was obsessed with money, and the others could be classed under the heading of either pride or laziness. Pride is the worst killer of pastoral effectiveness: rigid, cold, opinionated, narrow, pompous, ambitious, worldly pride, which smothers with clerical cloth all modesty, tact, and winsomeness.

What cheered me was the enormous number of devoted pastors who were giving all for Christ and their people. Let's get a composite picture of them. They speak the truth in love, take time to listen, and draw attention never to themselves but warmly toward Christ and the gospel. They rejoice with those who rejoice and weep with those who weep. They are all things to all men and cannot be shocked. Yet they are men set apart from other men, not by pride but by humility before the One who graciously called them into the ministry. They will eat with sinners and yet not be classed with them. They will hold their distance from cheap familiarity and yet meet soul to soul with the lowest. They condescend without being condescending. They will enter into the jovial heartiness of life and yet they will never wisecrack or tell a shady joke. They will be open, frank, and free but they will *never* betray a confidence. They will make their sermons practical by applying them to everyday situations but they will *never* use a pastoral experience as an illustration. They are clothed with I Corinthians 13; that is, with the Lord. They never give up hope for anyone's soul, because love hopeth all things. They preach as a dying man to dying men, as a living man to living men, and as a forgiven sinner to sinners needing forgiveness. They show in their person what holy love is, and give a new insight into what is meant by the God of patience, the God of hope, and the God of consolation. People in real trouble come to such a man. They tell others of the help they have found and quote to their children and grandchildren words that he never even remembers having said, though he acknowledges the thought. Such pastors are providential in the life of their whole congregation.

THE EFFECT OF PREACHING

A pastor's preaching will lead people to him for counseling or keep them away. It depends very much upon the color and shape of the sermon. If the color is blue and the shape is upside down, parishioners will either stay away or come for the wrong reasons. If the color and shape are right, people will either come to him eagerly or have no need to come.

The color

The three primary colors of attractive preaching are found in John 1:17: "The law was given by Moses, but grace and truth came by Jesus Christ."

Law is cold blue, the color of tempered steel, of the rifle barrel, of icy water, and of the unreachable sky. It is divine and necessary. As enshrined in the Ten Commandments and the Sermon on the Mount, it is an essential element of moral and spiritual life. But it is the hue of despair, the color of death, divinely condemning—necessary as surgeon's scalpel.

Grace is red, the red of lifeblood and sacrifice given and shed for the remission of sins. It is the color of passionate love, of the heart. It is the gospel.

Truth is sunshine yellow. It is the hue of reality, sincerity, practicality, and light.

The art of preaching is in the right mixture of these primary colors. There is no doubt which colors should predominate in a Christian sermon. "The law was given by Moses, *but* grace and truth came by Jesus Christ." "The law is holy and righteous and good . . . but by the works of the law shall no flesh be justified." In another famous passage Paul says that the glory of the law almost could be said to be no glory, by reason of the glory which excelleth.

Yet some sermons have a predominantly blue cast and thereby either discourage people from coming for counseling or lead them to come with warped ideas. Sleeping consciences, it is true, never produce genuinely peaceful hearts. They need rousing by the law. But we must ask ourselves: are our sermons essentially moralistic harangues and abstract dissertations on what the church ought to be, and how everybody ought to be a real Christian, or do they give real help for everyday life from the gospel? Are they wooing sermons, reaching broken hearts? Is acid blue the overcasting hue of our preaching? "The Lord hath anointed me to preach the gospel to the poor; to heal the broken-hearted, to preach deliverance to the captives, and recovering of sight to the blind, to set at liberty them that are bruised, to preach the acceptable year of the Lord." On the other hand, the present-day popular literature on Christian counseling tends to leave the blue color out entirely, raising a false antithesis. It is not a matter of leaving the blue out, but of making the red and yellow predominant.

The shape

The other important element of our preaching, in its effect upon pastoral counseling, is the shape of the sermon. What is emphasized? What is made large? What comes first? Is it right side up, or upside down?

Specifically, is the prime objective of our preaching and counseling holiness or happiness?

The dilemma we often face in preaching is that godliness is profitable and yet if we make profit the motive godliness vanishes. "Godliness *is* profitable unto all things, having promise of the life which now is, and of that which is to come." It results in the peace that passes all understanding, the true joy of life and even sometimes in prosperity. God never really allows a sacrifice, but heaps up compensation beyond measure. The gospel is not melancholy or repressive. Jesus often used the frank word, "reward." For the joy that was set before him, Christ endured the cross, despising its shame. When Peter said, "Lord, we have left all and followed thee. What, then, shall we have?" it might be expected that he would answer, "Peter, that is selfish thinking unworthy of a loyal follower." Instead he replied, "Verily I say unto you, There is no man that hath left house, or parents, or brethren, or wife, or children, for the kingdom of God's sake, who shall not receive manifold more in this present time, and in the world to come life everlasting."

So we are tempted to preach and to counsel, "Be religious and you will be happy," with the correlative, "If you are in bodily or spiritual need, there is something wrong with your religion." We encourage people, says Oscar Carlson, to accept Christ as a nice, accessible stepping stone to poise, power, popularity, peace, and prosperity. Religion becomes a tool for selfish ends. But it refuses to do so, and disappears, because it must be sovereign or it is nothing.

The resolving of the dilemma is in Jesus' words, "Seek ye *first* the kingdom of God and His righteousness, and all these things shall be *added* unto you." The skill of a real sermon is in giving it such shape that Jesus and His kingdom really do loom up as first and greatest, the happiness of life taking then its appropriate place as things "your heavenly Father knoweth that ye have need of."

> How can I chose but love Thee, God's dear Son,
> O Jesus, loveliest, and most loving One!
> Were there no heav'n to gain, no hell to flee,
> For what Thou art alone, I must love Thee.

We cannot merit the least of his mercies, but in the grace of the gospel we boldly lay claim upon his promises, for that is well pleasing unto him.

If the shape of a sermon is right, even the findings of the popular psychologists can take their place — like Dale Carnegie's six ways to make people like you:[2] "Become genuinely interested in other people; smile; remember that a man's name is to him the sweetest and most important sound in the English language; be a good listener, encouraging others to talk about themselves; talk in terms of the other man's interest; and make the other person feel important, doing it sincerely." How banal and nauseating these things sound when standing in crass selfishness by themselves. But if the shape of the sermon is right, these truths can have a place.

The Psalms are full of psychological truths placed in the right shaping. Study Psalm Thirty-two for its light on modern findings. Psalm Forty-two has a better method of "chasing the blues" than any mind-cure magazine on the stands. It says: in your feeling of isolation build a bridge of thankfulness to the past (verses four and six). Then build a bridge of faith and hope to the future, for God's promises are faithful as of old (verse eight). And finally, right where you stand, speak smartly and sharply to yourself (verse eleven).

Do these things even when dark thoughts keep coming up (the other verses of the Psalm). And yet we could never class the Psalm with worldly literature. It has a different shape. The worship of God is its very structure.

This is the kind of preaching that will bring Christian people to a Christian pastor's door. Even more important, it will make it unnecessary for many to come at all. They are already learning what the Word can mean to them.

THE EFFECT OF PARISH EDUCATION

Preaching is not formal education but it is a kind of teaching and therefore all that has been said concerning sermons applies as well to the formal nurture of the young in our parishes. But there are two aspects of youth training which are of special relevance to pastoral counseling.

"The Liberty of the Christian Man"

In counseling with youth, especially with adolescents, it is common to discover ambivalence in its most distressing form. For instance, a young man loves his father and yet hates him;

partly because the father has been domineering and partly because any youth tends to become rebellious during those trying years when he is gaining his selfhood and maturity.

It is a great help to youth, and to the pastor counseling him, if he has been taught Luther's "The Freedom of the Christian Man" and has studied in Luther League or church school the paradox of gospel liberty. The two statements of Luther's famous book, we remember, are: (1) Through faith in Christ, the Christian man is the lord of all things and subject to none. (2) Through love the Christian man is the servant of all and subject to all. The seeming contradiction is resolved in the fact that Christ the Lord died for us; the godly for the ungodly.

Youth needs a place to stand where he is independent of his parents and on his own—free. Fortunate is he, if he has found his freedom in Christ. That liberty includes not only fearless trust in the providence that governs all things, but also freedom from the guilt of his rebelliousness. From this liberty flows the love of Christ which takes away resentment against anyone, and substitutes a creative service of mankind, including parents first. Everybody needs this sense of ultimate freedom from the dominance of money, life, misfortune, the future, business, heredity, himself, his parents, his children, and even husband or wife. The history of disturbed minds is full of the false and illusory sources that are sought for, in the quest of this essential liberty. When it is found in the gospel of Christ, it produces not selfish exploitation and arrogance but "the love wherewith he has loved us." The expression of freedom is then love—examples of which are the deepest, most thoroughgoing and constructive in the history of the world: the *gesta Christi.*

Youth grounded in such education can learn to solve their

own problems. And when youth does come to the pastor with special perplexities and failures, the pastor has a background and a foundation for helpful counseling.

Interpersonal relations

As has been previously stated, inner, emotional, hidden conflicts are caused primarily by relations between people, according to the best findings of modern psychology. As H. S. Sullivan has written, "Psychiatry is the study of processes that involve or go on between people, under any and all circumstances."[3] If these social processes are healthy, psychiatry goes out of business. Much of Christian education in the parish is likewise concerned with the ability of people to get along with each other. In fact, Christianity is centered in the doctrine of the forgiveness of sins. Pastoral counseling is either found unnecessary or, if necessary, helpful when there has been thorough doctrinal and emotional training in this central teaching. Somehow the pastor must always get its implications into his counseling.

(1) *"If thy brother shall trespass against thee, go and tell him his fault between thee and him alone: if he shall hear thee, thou hast gained thy brother."* As pastors we know that we can solve at least fifty per cent of the interpersonal difficulties that are brought to us if we can get the parishioner to observe this simple rule. The trouble is that everybody else is told first. I have had that experience even with pastors and church councilmen. "Have you gone straight to *him* and talked it out?" I ask a complainer. "No, I thought the synod office was the place to straighten these things out!" "Well, try first going right to him and then come back and report." Often that settles

things completely. It will not always settle things but it is the first method to be tried in all love and honesty and courage.

It should be noted that the forgiveness of sins does not mean the overlooking of evil. "If thy brother trespass against thee, rebuke him." The world misunderstands forgiveness as appeasement or weakness or indifference. Sin is a horrible thing. It crucified Christ.

(2) *"If he repent, forgive him. And if he trespass against thee seven times in a day, and seven times in a day turn again to thee, saying, I repent; thou shalt forgive him."* Yea, saith the Lord, and seventy times seven. The Lord is not speaking just of rules but of the spirit: the willingness to forego pride and retaliation and vengeance and even recompense if only the repentance of the offender can be secured. In the search for that end, real psychological truth can be of help, such as Nathan used in turning David, Jesus in rescuing Peter, and the good bishop of *Les Misérables* in giving the stolen gold plate, and in addition the silver candlesticks, to reclaim Jean Valjean.

The process of the forgiveness of sins also involves the frank facing of our own faults. "If a man be overtaken in a fault, ye which are spiritual, restore such an one in the spirit of meekness; considering thyself, lest thou also be tempted." "With what judgment ye judge, ye shall be judged."

(3) *"The . . . brother . . . for whom Christ died."* That is how the enlightened Christian looks upon every man, woman, or child. It is an objective view which removes all subjective personal pride, greed, racial prejudice, tactlessness, boorishness, censoriousness, ruthlessness, and aggressive hostility. Even the "weak brother" is one for whom Christ died. "Wherefore, if meat make my brother to offend, I will eat no flesh while the

world standeth, lest I make my brother to offend," even though I think that eating meat offered to idols is no sin. Furthermore, the death of Christ for mankind places each individual so high that it is the best cure for any inferiority complex.

These are just three of the great dynamics of Christian faith, having their own autonomy over the hidden things of darkness within the human soul, valuable as a preventive against the need of counseling, or else valuable in its processes when it is needed. Fortunate are the youth who are grounded in the real meaning of love, keeping its romance but denying romanticism, experiencing its source in Christ, and working it out daily. Psychology says, "Work it out from yourself." Christianity says with Paul, "God works in you; now you work it out."

The Christian congregation, while not organized for the specific purpose, offers the best of "group therapy." It is the easiest place on earth to learn repentance and the forgiveness of sins. No one can in faith partake of the Sacrament of the Body and Blood of our Lord Jesus Christ for the forgiveness of sin, and then go out from the church with an unforgiving spirit. True, it is not accomplished in a moment. That is the reason for frequent church services, and for the continual fellowship of the church from the cradle to the grave. If we can have enough real Christian congregations all over the globe, think of the effect upon the inner conflicts of human hearts and even the destiny of nations!

THE EFFECT OF CONGREGATIONAL LIFE

Pastoral counseling cannot produce lasting results in a vacuum. The parishioner is not isolated, he is a member of a congregation. The pastor is not a free-lance therapist with a private practice, he is the head of a congregation, the shepherd of a flock. The corporate character of Christianity is often forgotten, especially in pastoral counseling. It should be the atmosphere of it. The very core of emotional trouble is the feeling of isolation.

Worship

In worship, the highest aim of soul cure is achieved: devotion that unifies life. But the public worship of the congregation doubles the effect because it is social, not merely individual. My father wrote, in his introduction to Strodach's *Manual on Worship,* "The man who 'goes to church' only for his personal spiritual profit has mistaken the character of a church service. His conception of worship is an entirely selfish one. He has failed to distinguish between private devotions and public worship, both of which are necessary. The Christian as he 'goes to church' should as far as possible cease to be an individual, should realize himself as an integral part of a congregation, of a fellowship of men, of the communion of saints. . . . The worshiper may rightly go beyond even the one congregation and recognize himself as in unity with all congregations of Christians . . . with the saints of all ages . . . in heaven. The effort to worship publicly in this manner will soon open up an increasing joy for the Christian, as he realizes the new richness of his worship." And, we might add, he will lose or prevent many self-centered neuroses.

The true effect of the Sacrament of the Lord's Supper lies in the same social direction. It is indeed the individualized Word, and the personal receiving of the real presence, for *me* and for the forgiveness of *my* sins. But the parishioner who ends there loses what he has gained.

No one else stressed more than Martin Luther the individual aspect. But listen to his further words: [4]

> *The significance or purpose of this sacrament is the fellowship of all saints* . . . of such a nature that all the spiritual possessions of Christ and His saints are imparted and communicated to him who receives this sacrament; again, all his sufferings and sins are communicated to *them,* and thus love engenders love and unites all. . . . It is like a city where every citizen shares with all the others the name, honor, freedom, trade, customs, usages, help, support, protection and the like, of that city, and on the other hand shares all the danger of fire and flood, enemies and death, losses, imposts and the like. . . . Whoever wrongs a citizen wrongs the entire city and all the citizens; whoever benefits one deserves favor and thanks from all the others.
>
> God gives us this sacrament, as though He said: "Behold, many kinds of sin assail thee; take this sign by which I give thee My pledge that sin assails not only thee but My Son Christ, and all His saints in heaven and on earth. Therefore, be bold and confident; thou fightest not alone; great help and support are round about thee."
>
> If any one be in despair, if he be distressed by his sinful conscience or terrified by death, or have any other burden on his heart, and desire to be rid of them all, let him go joyfully to the sacrament of the altar and lay down his grief in the midst of the congregation and seek help from the entire company of the spiritual body . . . lay down all misery and tribulation and put it on the congregation, and especially on Christ. . . . You must in turn also share the misfortunes of the congregation. . . . Lo, this is the benefit to be derived from this sacrament, this is the use we should make of it; then the heart cannot but rejoice and be comforted.

Do our people understand—have they been taught—these fundamental things? If so, they will not have to come to us for counseling. Or for right reasons they will come to us all the more. Somewhere, again, in the process of counseling this corporate idea must enter the picture for blessing. *"In this Christian Church,"* says the Catechism, "He daily forgives abundantly all my sins and the sins of all believers."

The same is true of baptism. Its comfort is, indeed, that God made a covenant with *me,* on which I can always lay claim. But its comfort is also that by it I became a member of the Body of Christ, a fellowship of heaven and earth, in newness of life.

To some extent the present pastoral counseling movement has been a healthy reaction against the exaggerated fad of the "social gospel," and toward ministry to the individual. But I think it needs for its very success the central truth of our corporate relations in Christ.

Many a troubled soul has said, "It was too painful for me, until I went into the sanctuary of God; then understood I."

The organizations

The Devil works hardest, I think, in the choir, the Brotherhood, the Women's Society, the Luther League, and the other organizations of the congregation. That is because these are the front-line trenches in the battle to put religious beliefs into actual work.

When you consider that sinful human beings make up our congregations, you wonder that these organizations can exist at all with their sublime aims. For one thing, it is a well-known, old, psychological truth that when two people are talking together, there are really six people. I think it was Oliver Wendell Holmes, in *The Autocrat of the Breakfast Table,* who said that when John and James are in conversation, there are three Johns and three Jameses. First there is the real John. Then there is John's idea about himself, quite different. And there is also James' idea of John, different from the other two. In like manner there is James himself, known only to his Maker, and James' idea of himself, which may bear little resemblance, and finally John's idea of James, which is something else again. When two people are talking, there are actually six all speaking at the same time because they involve both sides of the conversation. How can all confusion be kept out when six people are all speaking at once?

For another thing, there is a common idea that the church is a group of people who believe themselves better than other people. Sometimes church members harbor this misconception themselves and expect too much of each other. Someone is said to have approached Henry Ward Beecher with the question, "Is Mr. So-and-so a member of your congregation?" "Yes," replied Beecher, having a high regard for him. "Well, he cheated me!" "Oh," replied Beecher, "only once?"

Yet these organizations are indispensable to the pastor, not only in his church program, but in his pastoral counseling. He needs a *social context* for the working out of disturbed minds and hearts. He needs to give people something Christian to *do.* He needs a service group for those who have seen the need for an outreaching love. Happy is he if he has an organization willing to receive the lowliest and the most spiritually needy for Christ's sake. It is difficult, I know, to keep a church organization from becoming a select club, interested only in itself. It takes constant, understanding leadership to guide it into unselfish ends, as a part of the Body of Christ. But it can be done. And it is in these organizations, all over the territory of our church, that the stranger and the cripple and the dullard find a social place they could never have in any other kind of group.

Furthermore, it is in these organizations that the pastor can often explain most clearly his pastoral counseling ideals and hopes, enlisting their aid, and making partners of them.

Parish calling

There was a time fairly recently when parish calling was dubbed "door-bell pushing" and depreciated as a waste of time. Today there is a new appreciation of its importance, and our seminaries are stressing it. The pastoral counseling movement has done much to indicate its indispensable value. Writes Dr. Dicks, "Such calls are the heart of pastoral work, the foundation stones, the mother and father, the essence, the alpha and omega, all wrapped into one."

What he has in mind is not only sick calls, funeral visits, and the like, but the systematic shepherding of all the families of the congregation, calling at least once a year, district by district, and missing no one.

It is not easy, and that is one reason why we pastors don't do too much of it. John Watson (Ian Maclaren) said that it is a spiritual labor, intense and arduous, beside which reading and study are light and easy. "When the true pastor has been with ten families, and done his best by each, he comes home trembling in his very limbs and worn-out in soul." [5] But I have discovered that when he does come home, he can say every time (concerning at least some of the visits), "*That* call was certainly at the psychological moment."

Parish calling produces great riches. It is like putting money in the spiritual bank. It will bring more people to the pastor's office for counseling than any other one act. For it is not only during the visit that counseling is often done, but afterward.

All this presupposes that the visit is a truly pastoral one. To make it such, I have almost always offered prayer. That is my best safeguard. The call need not be long. It is more important to cover all the homes than to spend excessive time on a few, unless of course particular problems make a long call necessary or advisable. The mere presence of the pastor at the door reminds people of God, and it generally does not take him a long time after entering to sense the needs and glories of that home. The call is remembered through the year, making it easier than ever to approach the pastor with confidence and gladness.

The number of calls will be determined somewhat by the size of the congregation, but I have found that the best pastors, among those with large congregations, aim at a thousand a year, including the special visits upon the sick, the unfortunate, prospective members, and so on. No matter how many calls a pastor makes, he will get criticism from some members of the church council for not making more. The "callingest" minister I know got it. Nevetheless, the intuitive instinct of the church council on this subject is essentially correct, and the wise pastor acknowledges it, reports his calls, and does not let criticism ruffle him too much.

SUMMARY

It is an inspiring sight: a Sunday morning congregation. Where will you find its like for catholicity? Here are all kinds of people, old and young, rich and poor, wise and simple, male and female; people with German, Scandinavian, English, and a dozen other backgrounds; some who are able to hold their tempers and others not; some with the graces of good living and some with lowlier manners; some from large families and some from small, and some not married at all. Here are people working at a score of different daily tasks, in positions of responsibility or as hewers of wood and drawers of water. Every one has his particular cross, his special handicaps, and his peculiar temperament. But all are united in one great act of the worship of Christ!

Here is a fellowship that heals inner wounds. But if the pastor is the true shepherd, his people will also come to him one by one. For he exalts the Christ of the Nativity who is for all men, in their deepest needs.

In the words of Martin Luther, "Who are you? Who am I? Are we not all men? Aye, who should take this child to himself, if not all mankind? The angels do not need him; the devils do not want him. But we need Him, and He became man for our sake. For that reason it behooves us to accept Him with gladness, as the angel said, 'To *you* is born a Saviour!' "

V

HOW CAN I BECOME A BETTER COUNSELOR?

The Lord . . . is wonderful in counsel, and excellent in working.
ISAIAH 28:29

Reading is, of course, one of the ways to become a better counselor, even though it is admittedly not enough and perhaps overestimated. One cannot learn to swim by reading a book on the subject, but that helps.

In presenting the following selected bibliography on pastoral counseling I have listed only books that I have read. I have not mentioned those which I have read but found of lesser value and helpfulness. It is therefore a very personal choice, not to be considered authoritative in the slightest degree.

READING

Basic books

The Holy Bible. The Bible is the pastor's basic book in counseling, chiefly because in this place is found the way of salvation, the gospel, and the counsels of God. The pastor's task is to save souls, not just to cure the symptoms of their mental sickness. People in any condition need Christ above all, and in the Bible Christ reveals himself, in both Old Testament and New Testament. The Bible is the Word of God, and the Word of God is what the pastor has to give. It sets him apart from the psychologist or any other counselor. When the pastor neglects his Bible for other reading, he ceases to become a wonderful counselor and an excellent worker. He has allowed to become rusty the chief tool of his trade.

Furthermore, the Bible gives insight into the motives of the human heart and their ultimate outcome, as no other book. The life history of Adam and Eve has never been surpassed in this respect. Patriarchs and kings, prophets and psalmists, and the widest panorama of common human life, stretch out richly before us in the light of God. The perfect life in Christ, and the profound search of the soul in the epistles and in the apostolic church, show us what Christ can do for men, and therefore what we can do for men as shepherds under him.

The deepest need of human life is faith in Christ. Faith comes by hearing the Word of God. In pastoral counseling, therefore, we need to know the chief passages of the Bible by heart, and especially the guiding thought and spirit enshrined in the New Testament promises. Those who have found Christ and his Spirit will then use the Sermon on the Mount as the chart of their voyage through stormy spiritual seas, and as a practical compendium of Christian action. The Psalms will be the mirror of their inner conflicts and also the guide to resolve them.

A rich store of memorized verses will also be the main-spring of the pastor's prayers with those he counsels. The sheep will be fed and strengthened if he gives wisely and appropriately out of an understanding love, which in turn he has found in his own private Bible devotions. The comfort wherewith he has been comforted will be available for his people. They will follow in the steps which the Bible has lighted for *him* and avoid the pitfalls which *he* has learned from the Bible to escape.

For a beginner in the application of psychology to pastoral counseling, the best book is *The Pastor as a Personal Counselor* by the Rev. Carl J. Schindler, a Lutheran minister (Philadelphia: United Lutheran Publication House, 1942). It is not a new publication, but it gives in brief compass the essentials which never grow old.

Personal Problems of Everyday Living, by Travis and Baruch (New York: D. Appleton-Century, 1941) is a practical psychological guide which does not go at all into religion, but which is well-balanced and up-to-date on the scientific approach. It therefore is of use not as a guide but as a tool.

Counseling and Psychotherapy by Carl R. Rogers is the basic book on counseling used in the secular field, from which most of the present-day books on pastoral counseling derive their methodology. It does not mention religion. As a guide for the pastor, therefore, it leaves much to be desired. But every pastor will benefit from a reading of it because of its case histories, its recording of interviews, its systematic procedures, and its touch with life. It helped me more than the current books on pastoral counseling themselves. Rogers' more recent writing changes the term, "nondirective counseling" to "client-centered therapy."

A pastor who has mastered the above books will have an excellent equipment for this phase of his ministry. For further reading, the following works are of importance.

Pastoral counseling

John Sutherland Bonnell, minister of the Fifth Avenue Presbyterian Church, is a genius whom nobody could hope to emulate. His books are peculiarly his own. He was born in a mental hospital where his father was superintendent, and he was therefore reared in the atmosphere of psychological science and its immediate application. He has developed techniques which he is fitted to carry out, but which might go astray in the hands of many of us. His Christian approach and his great use of the Scriptures make his book stimulating and suggestive. He has a habit, for instance, of leaving a Bible verse, like a kind of prescription, with each sick parishioner, wisely chosen and given with a word of explanation. I recommend especially his *Psychology for Pastor and People.*

Two popular books, each entitled, *Pastoral Counseling,* have been written respectively by Seward Hiltner and his teacher, Carroll A. Wise. Enough has been said of them, I believe, to indicate their values and their shortcomings. Of the two books I prefer Wise's for its depth, clarity, and conciseness.

Pastoral Work and Personal Counseling by Russell L. Dicks, has also been referred to several times. It goes more widely into general pastoral work than the two above, but in general seems to me less valuable although Dr. Dicks has been a pioneer in this field. I prefer the work which he wrote with Richard R. Cabot, M.D., in 1936, entitled, *The Art of Ministering to the Sick* (Macmillan). It contains excellent practical advice to the minister in the sick room or hospital.

To keep oneself from becoming obsessed with the non-directive counseling technique, one should examine *Readings in Modern Methods of Counseling,* edited by Arthur H. Brayfield, where many opposing theories and methods are presented along with the Rogers school. Especially significant are the writings of Frederick C. Thorne given in this book.

Clinical training

The catalogues of the two systems of clinical training mentioned in a later section of this lecture will supply the best understanding of this topic, but profit may be derived also from *Clinical Pastoral Training* (Federal Council of Churches, 1945), a 162 page booklet containing the papers and findings of the National Conference on Clinical Training in Theological Education.

General Pastoral Work

From the Lutheran standpoint, the best book on practical theology is still Dr. G. H. Gerberding's *The Lutheran Pastor,* written in 1902, revised in 1915 and now reprinted by the Augsburg Publishing House, Minneapolis. It has some surprisingly modern viewpoints.

Oates' practical book, *The Christian Pastor* (Westminster, 1951), uses the most recent psychological discoveries sanely but does not always get at the heart of the gospel ministry. Standard books are *Pastoral Work* by Andrew W. Blackwood (Westminster, 1945) and the ever-inspiring *The Minister as Shepherd* by Charles E. Jefferson (Crowell, 1912). The Knubel-Miller Lectures were initiated by the profound yet crystal-clear talks of Dr. Walton H. Greever, published under the title, *The Minister and the Ministry* (Philadelphia: Board of Publication, ULCA, 1945).

Psychology

Freud's *Introduction to Psychoanalysis* has become as much of a classic in this field as Darwin's work in his, and pastors should read it, in spite of its nonreligious spirit and its exaggeration of sex. It is more worthy of reading than most of the books of his followers with the exception of Jung, Adler, Horney, Alexander and others, who greatly modified his emphases while retaining his basic methods.

Karen Horney's *Our Inner Conflicts,* and other writings have had a part in the shaping of the pastoral counseling movement because of her emphasis on character and because of the charm of her writing.

Erich Fromm is another eminent psychoanalyst whose writings have influenced the movement. In *Man for Himself* he shows clearly how the nature of love demands a moral and spiritual aim. Unfortunately his religion is rationalistic humanism. In his latest book on dreams he goes completely overboard, claiming that the stories of old are folk dreams with erotic meanings. The story of Jonah, for instance, is supposed to be the parable of one who could not love his fellowmen because he was always desiring to crawl back into the womb, symbolized by the ship's belly and the whale. What Fromm does to the story of Little Red Riding Hood is a caution!

To see how the theory and practice of psychoanalysis have changed through the years, one should read Clara Thompson's *Psychoanalysis: Evolution and Development* (Hermitage House, 1950).

Karl A. Menninger's *The Human Mind* is a 517 page book filled with case histories. It is valuable because of them, rather than for the theory he weaves around them. He views normal life from the standpoint of the abnormal, and often implies that because some people behave in a certain way, all people will. For instance, John the Baptist's fiery denunciations and call to repentance are explained as the result of John's own unconscious guilt feelings or secret hatred. Menninger's treatment of biblical incidents, as well as his explanation of historical characters and literary figures in general, make the book a reminder of Burton's *Anatomy of Melancholy,* a classic which no psychologist seems to dare to mention.

Psychology in general

A very good antidote for the extravagances of psychoanalysis, but which is appreciative of its important discoveries, is a textbook of the Harvard professor, Gordon W. Allport, *Personality; a Psychological Interpretation.* Prof. Allport is a practicing Episcopalian who stresses the autonomy of religious feelings. His little book, *The Individual and His Religion* (Macmillan, 1950) has an excellent psychological treatment of the doubts of young people, although the religious standpoint is pluralistic.

Edith M. Stern's, *Mental Illness: A Guide for the Family* (Commonwealth Fund, 1942) is a booklet which is helpful in clearing away popular prejudices and misunderstandings.

Psychology and religion

In this field there are, beside Allport's book, David E. Roberts', *Psychotherapy and a Christian View of Man* (C. Scribner's Sons, 1950), which is excellent but stops when it arrives at the real point; and Lewis J. Sherrill's *Guilt and Redemption,* which is most enlightening in the first half but is then marred by the author's venom against the use of any creeds and by his equating of faith and love.

Charles F. Kemp, in *Physicians of the Soul* (Macmillan, 1947), gives a history of pastoral counseling with emphasis on the modern development. John T. McNeill goes thoroughly into the reaches of the centuries in *A History of the Cure of Souls* (Harper, 1951). His book is scholarly and reverent. "In matters concerning the cure of souls," he writes, "the German Reformation had its inception." (One wonders what would have happened to the Reformation if Martin Luther, in his distress, had gone to a psychoanalyst instead of to a monastery and to Staupitz and finally to the Bible.)

Theology

The Quest for Holiness, by Adolf Köberle of Basel (Harper, 1936) is pure theology, but from a psychological viewpoint. It is a book that all pastoral counselors ought to read. Thoroughly modern, it goes to the heart of the important distinction for today between justification and sanctification, and the bearing of each on the actual experience of the soul beset by the moralism and self-salvation of our time.

Dr. Walton H. Greever's books are always clear and definite, and show what a living, important thing Christian theology is. *Human Relationships and the Church* (Revell, 1939), *The Work of the Lord* (Revell, 1937), and especially his latest little book, *Realities in the Christian Religion* (privately printed, 1951, and available through the ULPH) will keep the pastoral counselor clear on the implications of certain methods. Dr. Greever led in the foundation of the Knubel-Miller Lectures.

The great Swedish theologian, Anders Nygren, has written a monumental work, *Agape and Eros* (Macmillan, 1939), which has had great influence on the students of modern society in its dynamic aspects. Its subject is God's love toward us in relation to our love for each other, as Christian theology through the ages has developed the theme.

Although devotional rather than theological, Robert E. Speer's *The Principles of Jesus* gives a biblical study of Jesus' attitudes towards politics, forgiveness, friendship, marriage, children, property, the organization of society, the purpose of life, moral sanctions, and many other topics (Revell, 1902).

Special studies

Men, Women and God by A. Herbert Gray (Doran, 1922) is an older book but still seems to me the best guide on sex questions from the Christian point of view. Ernest R. Groves discusses *Christianity and the Family* (Macmillan, 1942). Well-known authors on marriage counseling are Emily Mudd, Paul Popenoe, and L. Foster Wood, whose *Harmony in Marriage* I have found excellent for young people.

Recently the United Lutheran Publication House has put out an excellent little book entitled *Love is No Luxury* by Marjory L. Bracher, a guide to Christian family living.

Older people are receiving more attention than ever before, and the Division of Welfare of the National Lutheran Council (50 Madison Ave., New York 10) has issued a valuable study by Henriette Lund, *Lutheran Services for Older People.* Maves and Cedarleaf's, *Older People and the Church* (Abingdon-Cokesbury, 1949) is well known.

Packets on *The Family* and on *Race Relations* can be ordered from the Board of Social Missions, 231 Madison Ave., New York 16. *Alcoholics Anonymous* (Works Publishing Co., 1939) explains the methods of that remarkable organization.

Fear, by John R. Oliver (Macmillan, 1931), is a fascinating story by one who is a clergyman, a doctor of medicine, and a psychiatrist.

Pastoral Care (Abingdon-Cokesbury, 1951, edited by J. Richard Spann) contains nineteen articles on the background and field for pastoral care written by pastors and chaplains who have gained prominence in each branch.

Mental Health in Modern Society (Commonwealth Fund, 1948) by T. A. C. Rennie and Luther E. Woodward, a Lutheran minister, has a chapter on pastoral counseling and church life.

Magazines

The pastoral counseling movement has produced two magazines. One is *The Journal of Pastoral Care,* a quarterly sponsored jointly by the two clinical training agencies in the United States. Subscriptions are $3.00 a year and should be sent to the business manager, the Rev. Frederick C. Kuether, Council for Clinical Training, 2 East 103rd St., New York 29, N. Y.

The other is *Pastoral Psychology,* published monthly except July and August by the Pulpit Digest Publishing Co., 159 Northern Blvd., Great Neck, N. Y., at $3.00 a year.

I prefer the first. It is the official journal of a responsible group, centered more on the religious and Christian aspects, and containing more articles that are of lasting value to the pastor. The second is a commercial project, but it has an eminent editorial advisory board which includes Dr. Woodward and Dr. Krumbholz and is headed by Seward Hiltner. It is more psychological than pastoral.

CLINICAL TRAINING

Another way offered to ministers and theological students

to improve their pastoral counseling is clinical training.

There are two outstanding agencies that handle it. The Institute of Pastoral Care is under the direction of Chaplain James H. Burns, Massachusetts General Hospital, Boston 14, Mass. It is supported by seminaries, individuals, and fees. It is an organization that has many training centers, including Boston, Chicago, Portland, Ann Arbor, and Worcester, to name those where summer schools are conducted. These summer schools have six- and twelve-week courses. Regular sessions are held during the rest of the year.

The other is the Council for Clinical Training, the Rev. Frederick C. Kuether, director, 2 East 103rd St., New York 29, N. Y. It is similarly set up, and its training centers include New York, Elgin, Independence (Iowa), Manteno (Ill.), Concord (N. H.), Trenton, Norristown, Norwich (Conn.), Philadelphia, Washington, D. C., Columbia (S. C.), Little Rock, Lorton (Va.), Chillicothe, El Reno, and St. Charles (Ill.).

At these places the students live, working under the supervision of a chaplain or his assistant. The institutions are general hospitals, mental hospitals, or corrective institutions. The students attend staff meetings, learn hospital routine, assist in recreation and religious services, interview patients under supervision, write reports, and receive criticism. As they advance, certain patients receive their special attention. They learn how to co-operate with doctors, and also with social agencies and the home. They attend classes and lectures. The purpose is not primarily to train specialists, but to give seminarians and ministers a knowledge of the deeper aspects of human nature so that they will become more effective pastors.

Many of our Lutheran leaders have had a vital part in this project. At least seven of the centers have a Lutheran as supervisor. It is estimated that 2,500 pastors and seminarians of all denominations have taken this training in the past twenty years.

I have interviewed many students who have had this experience, as well as several supervisors, and without exception find them enthusiastic. They are unanimous in this conclusion, too: it all depends on the character and spirituality of the supervisor. That is what is probably back of the reserve with which some seminary presidents look upon the idea of clinical training. Even the presidents and professors who have had a formative part in the movement, and are today its firmest supporters, believe "that it all depends." Some of them are not in favor of it for *all* seminarians and pastors, and especially not for such as tend toward morbidity.

As one president writes, "Some instructors were out-and-out Freudians, drumming away at their theories *ad nauseum.* Some of our students were all upset when they came back to the seminary. . . . I would not favor clinical training for all students. There are dangers: the tendency of the student to become too introspective and introverted; the tendency of the student to consider all people cases needing unusual treatment, and to look upon all members of a congregation as abnormal; the tendency to emphasize psychological methods and findings at the expense of revealed truths and theology; and the tendency to look down on others who do regular pastoral work as being formal, well-intentioned and assiduous but not scientific." Yet this president has had first-hand part in the development of the training, and feels that for mature and emotionally stable students it has value, under proper leadership. The president of a second, large Lutheran seminary which is fully abreast of the movement expresses almost exactly the same thoughts in his letter to me.

HOW THE SEMINARIES STAND

I wanted to know how our seminaries stood on pastoral counseling in general, and received replies from all nine of them. Did they have a place for it in their curriculum? Excerpts from their answers follow.

Philadelphia Seminary. "Pastoral counseling is becoming an increasingly useful tool in the service of the Church. A considerable amount of time is given to it in the course on Pastoral Work required of all students, and in an elective."

Gettysburg Seminary. "Our seminary gives considerable teaching on the subject. There is a separate course on it. (Dr. Bertha Paulssen is an authority on the psychological phase of theology.) We have had many men in institutions for clinical training."

Northwestern Seminary. "Our seminary offers an elective, over and above ordinary pastoral care and *Seelsorge.* We also have an eleven-hour course on specialized pastoral counseling, including that type generally taught for clinical training and institutional and hospital work, under the Rev. F. M. Norstad of our Minnesota Lutheran Welfare Society. Some of our graduates and undergraduates have taken clinical training in Chicago under Dr. Granger Westberg, and others at Boston."

Hamma Divinity School. "We have established courses on the subject for several years, and have been fortunate in having on our faculty Dr. T. A. Kantonen, who was well trained in this field in Boston in the earlier years of the movement and has followed it ever since. He offers very popular and helpful courses in the field. We relate the students to local churches and the Inner Mission. A local Mental Hygiene Society offers clinical opportunity."

Chicago Seminary. "We think the movement is important and that the seminary must teach it as thoroughly as possible. We have made arrangements by which every one of our students does some work in hospitals under a trained supervisor, which we think better than a few students getting more extended experience. We do not see how more training in counseling can be given by adding new courses to the already overcrowded curriculum. It seems that to be of genuine value it has to take its place in an integration of insights, in which it both receives and sheds light on the whole of life and work."

Southern Seminary. "We give what I consider to be a fairly accurate course in Pastoral Counseling in the field of Pastoral Theology. We do not go too deeply into the subject under the head of psychological emphases. This would require a highly trained specialist. On connection with clinical training, our students go regularly to the State Hospital where they have practical experience in observation under the direction of physicians, and especially the Rev. Obert Kempson, its Chaplain."

Saskatoon Seminary. "We present a one-semester course entitled, 'Pastoral Psychology,' dealing with various attitudes and complexes and showing how a pastor should attempt to cope with them. As a text we use *Pastoral Psychology* by Stoltz. Some attention to pastoral counseling is also given in our course entitled, 'Pastoral Theology,' and practical experience is provided through supervised visits to various local institutions."

Waterloo Seminary. "Our faculty is so small that it is impossible for us to give the emphasis to pastoral counseling which it rightly deserves. Concepts developed in descriptive psychology (rather than explanatory) can serve as auxiliaries in understanding human nature and in providing channels for healing. It can and must serve the Word."

Central Seminary. (Because of administrative changes, final answer could not be included, but the Seminary is known to be thoroughly aware of the opportunities of the field.)

The National Lutheran Council. Dr. Clarence E. Krumbholz' Division of Welfare has drawn up a suggested curriculum for seminaries in the field of pastoral counseling, worked out by the Lutheran Advisory Council on Pastoral Care, under the leadership of the Rev. Carl R. Plack, director of Chaplaincy Service, and including programs of clinical work. The Advisory Council believes that clinical training opportunities should be provided, and has adopted certain minimum standards.

What is needed is a graduate school which will guide and supply leaders for the expanding opportunities.

I believe that local pastoral groups could pool their experiences on counseling, and that pastors who have special training could be of great help to their fellow clergymen.

GROWING IN GRACE

Better than reading, study, clinical training, and experience is the pastor's inner growth in grace and in the knowledge of our Lord Jesus Christ, if he is to be a more effective counselor.

His person is important. Let there be no mistake about that. All schools of psychology stress the effect on counseling of the personal life of the counselor and of his inner make-up.

It is acknowledged as the heart even of the Rogers method. One of the greatest psychoanalysts says, "Neurotics never get well for their own sake. They get well to please the physician. They do it as a favor to him." One of the biggest problems of institutions of mental care is to get staff members who are themselves healthy in heart and soul. Are pastors an exception to this emphasis? Hiltner in his latest book says it well, "It is not true that the best approach to improving our counseling is merely learning more and more about the people we try to help. Fully as important is the discovery of hidden strength and obstacles in ourselves." [1]

Do we take offense easily, feel slighted, like to dominate, become envious when others are honored, get concerned more for ourselves than for others, feel persecuted? Let every pastor watch for the things that raise his blood pressure, and examine them. Is fear back of them? Or conscience? Are we growing in grace? Are we becoming Christian persons?

After all, the glorious gospel of the blessed God was committed to *our* trust. God always chose persons for his task, and revealed himself both to them and through them. Nothing can take the place of a person: not even radio and phonograph records and television. The personally preached Word, with personal counseling and teaching and helping form the saving instruments of God's mercy. He uses these earthen vessels.

This truth is terrifying. The terror is removed (as well as any pride which may creep in) if first of all we will be ourselves in counseling. I have found as a synod president that some of the men who succeed above others in their pastoral work are not always the most brainy, or the best read, or possessed of the glamor of "personality" and "charm." They are themselves. A pastor makes the best counselor if he is natural. Each works out his own best method. Each has unique possibilities.

Another preventive of terror is the conviction that when someone comes to you for counseling, God has put him there. Need we feel fear of them or of ourselves if that is the case? Will not God give all the necessary grace for the occasion if we really believe this? "Those whom thou hast given me" was Jesus' identification of his disciples. (It is a good way to think about church councils, too, when personalities become difficult.)

RESOURCES OF THE SPIRIT

But chief among the pastor's means for the improvement of his person, and for the release of his terror and pride when he thinks about it, are the resources of the spirit.

After all, the greatest of counselors is the Holy Spirit. It is he who changes us and changes others. When people are helped, we do not do it—he does it. Let him work without the interference of our feverishness and anxiety.

Daily devotions and prayers consequently become the absolute necessity of the pastor. "If a man neglect his Bible," said Moody, "he may ask God to use him, but there is not much for the Holy Spirit to work with."

I commend to you not only regular prayer, and special times of fervent adoration, supplication, intercession, and thanksgiving, but also the "flash" prayer before a pastoral counseling interview and at times during it.

The pastor's person becomes refulgent at the very moment when he realizes that God is simply working through him—that God does the work. There is a statue of Phillips Brooks in front of his old church on Copley Square in Boston. He is preaching with evident fervent power. The reason is that back of him is the statue of Christ, and the figure of Christ is resting its hand upon the shoulder of Phillips Brooks. It is as if Christ were saying, "Tell them I love them. Tell them the Way." It is Brooks "bringing the truth through personality," but it is really Christ who is preaching.

Here is the guide and solace also for counseling. God is using our person, but it is he who counsels effectively, and he who works the wonders. We shall not be cast down over seeming failures, nor shall we rejoice that the devils are subject unto us. We shall rather rejoice because our names are written not on earth but in heaven. Let a man so account of us: not as psychiatrists, and not as professionals and not as wonder workers, but as ministers of Christ and stewards of the mysteries of God.

His name was called Wonderful Counselor! Our counseling takes on the same quality when he speaks through us.

REFERENCES

I *What is the Pastoral Counseling Movement?*

1. Anton T. Boisen, *The Exploration of the Inner World* (New York: Harper & Bros., 1938). Used by permission.
2. Flanders Dunbar, *Mind and Body: Psychosomatic Medicine* (New York: Random House, 1947).
3. Karen Horney, *Our Inner Conflicts* (New York: Norton, 1945), pp. 28ff.
4. Carl R. Rogers, *Counseling and Psychotherapy* (Boston: Houghton Mifflin, 1942), p. 176.
5. Seward R. Hiltner, *Pastoral Counseling* (New York: Abingdon-Cokesbury, 1949).
6. Carroll A. Wise, *Pastoral Counseling* (New York: Harper & Bros., 1951), pp. 73ff. Used by permission.
7. Carl G. Jung, *Modern Man in Search of a Soul* (New York: Harcourt Brace, 1932).
8. R. S. Bonnell, *Psychiatry for Pastor and People* (New York: Harper & Bros., 1948), p. 31.
9. A. H. Brayfield, ed., *Readings in Modern Methods of Counseling* (New York: Appleton-Century-Crofts, 1950).
10. Wise, *op. cit.*, p. 154.
11. Wise, "When is Counseling Religious?" in *Journal of Clinical Pastoral Work,* Vol. II, No. 2, Summer, 1949, pp. 88f.
12. Karl Heim, *The Church of Christ and the Problems of the Day* (New York: C. Scribner's Sons, 1935), p. 82. Used by permission.
13. Wise, *op. cit.*, p. 165.
14. Anton T. Boisen, *op. cit.*, p. 237.
15. Hiltner, *op. cit.*, pp. 30ff.

II *How Much Psychology Should a Pastor Know?*

1. Gordon W. Allport, *Personality, a Psychological Interpretation* (New York: Holt, 1937).
2. William Ernest Hocking, *Science and the Idea of God* (Chapel Hill: University of North Carolina Press, 1944), p. 30. Used by permission.
3. Erich Fromm, *Man for Himself* (New York: Rinehart, 1947).
4. J. S. Wechsler, *The Neurologist's Point of View* (New York: Fischer, 1945), p. 59.
5. Harry Stack Sullivan, *Conceptions of Modern Psychiatry* (William Alanson White Psychiatric Foundation, 1947), p. v.
6. G. H. Gerberding, *The Lutheran Pastor* (Minneapolis: Augsburg Publishing House, 1902), p. 382.
7. Karl A. Menninger, *The Human Mind* (New York: Knopf, 1945), pp. 279 ff. Used by permission.
8. William S. Sadler, *The Theory and Practice of Psychiatry* (St. Louis: Mosby, 1936), chap. 73.
9. Allport, *op. cit.*, p. 12.
10. Heim, *op. cit.*, pp. 89 ff.

11. Lewis J. Sherrill, *Guilt and Redemption* (Richmond: John Knox Press, 1945), pp. 70 ff.
12. Menninger, *op. cit.*, p. 449.
13. Hocking, *op. cit.*, p. 43.
14. Wise, *op. cit.*, pp. 82, 97,9.
15. Russell L. Dicks, *Pastoral Work and Personal Counseling* (New York: Macmillan, 1944), pp. 9 f. Used by permission of The Macmillan Company.
16. Boisen, *op. cit.*, p. 268.
17. Otto A. Piper, "Justification and Christian Ethics" in *Theology Today*, 1951.
18. Dicks, *op. cit.*, p. 50.

III *What Shall I Tell People?*

1. J. Obert Kempson, "The Parish Minister's Care of the Mentally Ill" in *Journal of Pastoral Care*, Vol. 5, No. 3 (Reprints available from the author, State Hospital, Columbia, S. C.).
2. Dicks, *op. cit.*, p. 85.
3. Erich Lindemann, "Symptomatology and Management of Acute Grief" in *Journal of Pastoral Care*, Vol. 5, No. 3

IV *Why Don't People Come To Me?*

1. Lee R. Steiner, *Where do People Take Their Troubles?* (Boston: Houghton Mifflin, 1945).
2. Dale Carnegie, *How To Win Friends and Influence People* (New York: Pocket Books, 1936), p. 104.
3. Sullivan, *op. cit.*, introduction.
4. Martin Luther, *A Treatise on Christian Liberty*, pp. 301 ff. and *A Treatise Concerning the Blessed Sacrament*, pp. 10 ff. in *The Works of Martin Luther* (Holman edition)Vol. II.
5. Ian Maclaren, quoted by Charles F. Kemp, *Physicians of the Soul* (New York: Macmillan, 1947), p. 95.

V *How Can I Become a Better Counselor?*

1. Seward W. Hiltner, *The Counselor in Counseling* (New York: Abingdon-Cokesbury, 1952).

Type used in this Book
Body, 12 on 14 and 10 on 11 Garamond
Display, Garamond